THE ONION'S DARK CORE

A LITTLE BOOK OF POETRY TALK

THE
ONION'S
DARK CORE

A LITTLE BOOK OF POETRY TALK

David
Bottoms

Press 53
Winston-Salem

Press 53, LLC
PO Box 30314
Winston-Salem, NC 27130

First Edition

Cover design by Kevin Morgan Watson

Author photo by Rachel Bottoms

Index by Alexa Selph

Library of Congress Control Number: 2010905305

Printed on Acid-Free Paper
ISBN 978-1-935708-02-5

*this little book and everything else
is for Kelly and Rachel*

Contents

1. Essays

2. Interviews

Acknowledgments

"Literature and the Inevitable" first appeared in *The Atlanta Journal-Constitution*.

"Articulating the Spirit: Poetry, Community, and the Metaphysical Shortwave" was delivered as the Georgia Humanities Lecture for 2002 and published in a monograph by the Georgia Humanities Council.

"Thirst and the Writer's Sense of Consequence" first appeared in *The Kennesaw Review* and was reprinted in *Best of the Web 2008* from Dzanc Books.

"What the Graveyard Says: A Thought on the Consequence of Place" was delivered as the Ferrol Sams Lecture at Mercer University for 2005.

"The Poetry of Bridges: Growing Up Small-town, Gazing Toward Atlanta" was commissioned by the U.S. Department of State and published in *American Cities and Authors*.

"The Poetry Receiver: An Interview With David Bottoms" first appeared in *Atlanta Review*.

"Fishing from the Poetry Boat: A Conversation With David Bottoms" appeared in *The Southern Quarterly*.

"The Onion's Dark Core: A Conversation With David Bottoms" appeared in *Southbound: Interviews with Southern Poets* (Columbia: University of Missouri Press, 1999), ed. Ernest Suarez.

"A Baked Tortilla Scorched With the Face of Christ" originally appeared in *Five Points: A Journal of Literature and Art*.

"Shooting Rats at the Bibb County Dump," "Sign for My Father, Who Stressed the Bunt," and "The Desk" are reprinted from *Armored Hearts: Selected and New Poems* (Port Townsend: Copper Canyon Press, 1995).

ESSAYS

LITERATURE AND THE INEVITABLE

For almost five hours last night, I watched a man dig a grave, a guy I know, a decent man who occasionally gets himself into trouble trying to help people. This was in a small rural cemetery in west Cobb County, and my friend was digging a grave to bury the young woman lying in the bed of his truck. She'd been dead, I think, for almost a week when he found her body at the bottom of a well. She was taped up inside two large black garbage bags, and for all the duct tape covering the seams, the stench made us hunt a spot upwind. I won't go into the reasons why my friend refused to call the sheriff and wanted to bury her in that out-of-the-way graveyard, but will say only that watching him was a curious and an eerie thing. Everything about the deed seemed intensified—each slight grunt before a shovelful of dirt spilled onto the tarp we'd bought at Sears, the shadows of the headstones sloping toward the woods, even the barking of the tree frogs in the dark of those woods. Something about his desperation colored the whole horrible event, so that to me, at least, it seemed almost heroic, strangely beautiful.

The man who dug that grave finished his work before sunrise, maybe four-thirty or five, got into his truck and drove away, and I switched off my word processor and leaned back in my chair. I thought about what I'd written—another graveyard scene—and wondered again about this obsession with cemeteries.

A typically Southern thing, and with me long standing. One critic somewhere even tagged me a member of the "new graveyard school." I didn't know there was one—we haven't had any meetings—but I have haunted more than my share of cemeteries and have written a number of poems about those ramblings. I even set a fair amount of my second novel, *Easter Weekend*, inside an open grave in Rose Hill Cemetery in Macon, Georgia. So the tag seems fair enough.

The fact is, if there is a new graveyard school in the South or anywhere else, it's quite a large one. The Southern poet Dave Smith has written in an essay that there are only two subjects for poetry: life and death. He's at least half right. Actually, I think there is only one, and every theme in literature, remote as the connection might seem, is a variation of it. The world, of course, is simply an infinite variation on death, and therefore so is the word. I mean that in this sense. One of the most fascinating and instructive books I've ever read is Ernest Becker's *The Denial of Death*, which won the Pulitzer for nonfiction in 1975. Becker's notion, much simplified, is that every aspect of our personality is a lie whose function is the denial of the one absolute truth in our lives. Perhaps his best metaphor is an onion—all the aspects of our personality are like the layers of an onion, and when we peel these layers away they reveal the core, which is our one undeniable truth. Of course, these layers, these lies of the personality, are necessary and healthy because without them emptiness and despair would quickly overwhelm us. We wouldn't be able to function in the world. Nevertheless, they remain lies, avoidances, denials. But here's the thing. These denials, these personal dreams and passions, are the raw material out of which we make poetry, drama, and fiction. In this sense then, all imaginative writing has at its core our one undeniable fact. Or to say it another way, under every piece of literature lies a grave.

Writers who are drawn to this grave and approach it more directly than others are likely to be called melancholy or morbid. In American literature, many of these folks have been Southern. They are likely to be called prophets of gloom, sowers of despair, perhaps even to be associated with new graveyard schools. But the truth may be something closer to the opposite. In the best poetry and fiction, something interesting happens. Literature can achieve a curious emotional bargain with death. Not that death ever negotiates, of course. Nevertheless, a kind of bargain can still be struck, good things wrenched from despair. We may get in our slice of the bargain understanding, resignation, empathy, and I might even say beauty. In the presence of this beauty, we may even find affirmation and transcendence.

One of my favorite examples of this is a poem by Robert Penn Warren called "After the Dinner Party." As the situation unravels for us an old couple sits at their dining room table late at night. The dinner is over, the guests are gone, the fire is burning down in the fireplace. Everything about the scene suggests an ending of things. They talk of the past, of their children who are away and building their own lives. It's painfully clear that they understand the past is gone and that they can expect no real future. The woman snuffs out the candles and they sit quietly in the last light of the fire. Then Warren writes: "Soon the old stairs/Will creak to the briefness of light, then true weight of darkness, and then/ That heart-dimness in which neither joy nor sorrow counts." Now what could be darker, bleaker, than this truth? No joy in the past or the future, no sorrow, no human emotion will stop or delay the inevitable. Then he writes in the last line, "Even so, one hand gropes out for another, again." And there it is, an amazing affirmation—not of the past or the future, but of the only thing left, the moment.

This is what real art can do, all art. What else is the blues but turning trouble into something good? Perhaps this explains something about the wealth of great literature in the South. Trouble, of course, isn't unique to our region, but ours has been historically the most volatile in America, the place where much of our national identity has been violently molded. Art transcends where there is a need for transcendence.

ARTICULATING THE SPIRIT:
POETRY, COMMUNITY, AND THE
METAPHYSICAL SHORTWAVE

A few days after the attack on the Pentagon and the Twin Towers of the World Trade Center, I received a phone call from Lea Donosky, who was then the excellent editor of the @ *Issue* section of the *Atlanta Journal-Constitution* and is currently the excellent editor of the Sunday edition. Over the past week, she said, the paper had received dozens and dozens of poems from its readers—poems in rhyme and meter, poems in free verse, angry poems, grief-stricken poems, but no poem they cared to publish. Still, she thought, people seemed to be expressing a need for poetry. Might I be able to get something into lines that she could run in their Sunday edition? Two things struck me immediately as not a little bit startling. First, I was jolted by the notion of a major newspaper in America commissioning a poem for publication, a fairly gutsy maneuver in journalism. Second, I was no less surprised that in a time of national distress so many people would turn to a genre that, in America, has never been popular, at least not in the commercial sense. Still poetry was, according to Donosky, the chosen mode of expression—no stories came in, no essays. Stories and essays generally take up more space, of course, and poetry affords us a more muscular and compact expression. All of that is true, but I suspect much more is at work here than a concern for economy of expression, much that has to do with world-view, with a different way of approaching the world than our usual nine-to-five stance. When we encounter the poem, as writer or reader, something unique is required of us, and we must call up aspects of our psyche that often lie buried under those more rational talents we use to negotiate the everyday traffic of the world. Ed Hirsch, in a marvelous book called *How to Read a Poem and Fall in Love With Poetry*, calls the poem "a soul in action." "The spiritual life," he writes, "wants articulation—it wants embodiment in language." True enough. The spiritual life needs articulation. It needs to find a voice, but why poetry? What's very important is how poetry, of all literary genres, provides the most natural vehicle for the spirit. This concerns three particular aspects of poetry—the way poems come into the world, the way they deliver their message to us, and the nature of that message itself.

* * *

Poetry, of course, is an immense genre, and folks tend to see it, dissect it, and categorize it in many different ways, which depend ultimately, like all art, on one's fundamental world-view. This is all a way of saying that I can speak only of the poem as I know it. In doing so I'll probably do best to start at the beginning and acknowledge outright that poetry, for me, has always involved an element of the other-worldly.

This, no doubt, is due in large part to the particular, if not unusual, way I first came to poetry, or perhaps I should say, to the particular way poetry first came to me. If there was anything strange about my childhood, it was my love of books. I was born in Canton, Georgia, in 1949, and grew up there in the 1950s and 1960s. Canton then was just about as American a place as I can imagine—a place both beautiful and bleak for its lack of anything we might call "the arts"— two traffic lights, a courthouse built of Georgia marble, a post office, a scattering of stores up and down Main Street. There was a library, yes, old and tottering at the head of the town, a beautiful Victorian ramshackle that radiated in its decades of dust all the mysteries of time, culture, and place. But by the time I was seven or eight years old and susceptible to its attractions, the city fathers tore it down and built in its place a very utilitarian brick and concrete box, which looked like it should have had machine gun turrets on the roof.

Often I hear folks repeat the old saw that the best way for a child to acquire a love of reading is for the parents to read to that child and to read themselves. A father or a mother sitting comfortably in an easy chair, with an open novel in hand, is said to be a powerful model. This may be, but I wouldn't know. Not once in my entire childhood did I ever see my father or my mother sit down in the living room and pick up a book for the purpose of leisure. They simply were not book people. Television was their only entertainment. After a hard day at Holcomb Chevrolet or the Jones-Hendrix clinic, they had little energy for anything else.

Most of the books in our house belonged to me. Most of those were school books. My Granny Ashe had ten or so novels on a small bookshelf in her living room—two of those were *Gone with the Wind*, a hardback and a paperback—and my uncle had a book club edition of the novels of the Western writer Zane Grey. Other than the King James Bible that was just about the entire library of my extended family.

This is not to poor-mouth my "raising," as they say where I come from, or to suggest that I suffered any childhood deprivations, a notion that would horrify my mother. Indeed, I was blessed with an exceptionally happy childhood in which I was surrounded by a family of strong and loving Southern Baptists, people who lived what they believed. I mention that it was not a reading family merely to point out a curious fact concerning my relationship to books and the call I felt them issue.

One great advantage I did enjoy, however, was my mother's encouragement. Though she didn't read herself, she understood well the importance of an education and pushed me to develop an interest in books. She took me to the county library and to McClure's Bookstore, a wonderful little shop owned by my second-grade teacher. It was a quaint and dimly lit place filled with many of the classics one would expect a child to read—Mark Twain, Jules Verne, Lousia May Alcott—as well as the more "with-it" adventures of the Hardy boys, Tom Swift, and Nancy Drew. And then there were those first teachers at Canton Elementary School— Ms. Jones, Ms. McClure, Ms. Cobb, the Bozeman sisters— extraordinary teachers, who emphasized not only the importance, but the joy of reading.

Poetry, however, came from another source. I'm sure I must have run across the usual sort of children's verse that everybody bumps into along the way—Robert Louis

Stevenson, Lewis Carroll, and such—but I don't recall them. My earliest memories concerning a language I might call poetic go back to the mid-1950s and a basement room in the Canton First Baptist Church. I still recall vividly the rows of little round-backed chairs facing the blackboard where the children of the Sunday school's Primary Department met as a group to sing before they broke up into smaller classes for Bible stories. There, in that basement room, I first encountered the beauty, praise, and anguish of the Psalms, a poetry that has addressed for thousands of years the deepest of human concerns.

Even then, as a seven- or eight-year-old boy, I felt something in that antique and exotic English intimating the other-worldly, the sacred. Remembering that now puts me in mind of a bumper sticker I saw once on a pickup truck in Cobb County. It read, "If it ain't the King James, it ain't the Bible." I might not go quite that far, but I must confess that I still feel much the same way about the music of the King James. What poet could argue with this heart-torturing lament from Psalm 102: "For I have eaten ashes like bread, and mingled my drink with weeping./ Because of thine indignation and thy wrath: for thou has lifted me up, and cast me down./ My days are like a shadow that declineth; and I am withered like grass." Or the equally beautiful and infinitely more hopeful message of Psalm 23: "The Lord is my shepherd; I shall not want./ He maketh me to lie down in green pastures: he leadeth me beside the still waters."

Another source of poetry that washed across me in great waves of language and imagery were those hymns we sang in church. "Rock of Ages, cleft for me, let me hide myself in Thee." Or another of my favorites, "Shall we gather at the river, where bright angel feet have trod?" My Grandma Bottoms, who had no great talent for music, used to croak out two old gospel songs, one after the other, almost constantly as she did her housework—"I'm gonna lay down my burdens, down by the riverside" and "Some glad morning when this life is o'er, I'll fly away." Now there's a thought.

These psalms and songs, then, were my first experiences with language as art, with imagery riding waves of rhythm. And they were also, certainly, my first encounters with the figurative meanings of language. Toward water imagery and its capacity for metaphor I was drawn most especially. Everyone, it seemed, was always crossing some body of water, the Jordan River or the crystal sea. And peace was like a river, the Gospel itself like a ship. A person's life, I began to understand, is a journey, a setting out and a crossing over, which—if led the right way—ends at that most desirable destination when, as the bluegrass musician Carter Stanley phrases it, "the great ship shall anchor in the harbor of love."

* * *

Little wonder then that I have always seen the poem pointing toward something beyond the mundane noise of our everyday lives, and that I don't hesitate to call poetry the most natural voice for the spirit. But where precisely does poetry come from and how does it suggest to us meanings that transcend the literal stage props of the world?

A few days before he died, I had a long telephone conversation with my friend James Dickey. We rarely talked over the phone about poetry, but this time he wanted to talk about that, and about his own poetry. He told me that he was dying, and he wanted to know what I thought of his work. I told him, as I had always told him, that he was the champ, and I reminded him of a lunch we'd had several years earlier with the fiction writer Peter Taylor and a story Taylor had told about his close friend, Robert Lowell. Lowell, he'd said, was a very jealous man, and he was jealous of no one more than he was jealous of James Dickey. There was a deep pause then on Jim's end of the line. He was remembering that lunch perhaps, or weighing the comment. Then he said something that has stuck with me. He said, "The goal of the poet is to make the world more available." Lowell's flaw was that he had not made the world at large more available, but only the world of Robert Lowell. In his selfishness, Dickey thought, Lowell had gotten between the reader and the world.

The goal of the poet certainly should be to make the world more available. The reader wants to get at the world, to get into the world, to experience all the world has to offer. Oddly enough, however, and even more importantly, the world wants to get into the reader. This seems, at first, a rather strange notion, the world exhibiting a desire to communicate, a need to express itself, as though the world itself were some sentient and all-encompassing creature. Robert Penn Warren, however, loved to say that the world is always trying to tell the poet something, and that notion becomes slightly less bizarre if we posit behind the world a sentient Creator, which I am always happy to do. Years ago I used to think of the world as whispering its secrets, and the poet as something of an eavesdropper, a spy, a secret agent straining to hear, but more and more now I think of the world as shouting, yelling, screaming at us from all angles, virtually every moment of our lives—a place bursting with meaning, with overlooked significance, crazy for an audience, like a maniac on a street corner frantic to grab our attention, so eager to get all of its messages across that the truly significant are very often lost among the mundane and trivial. And therein we find the origins of the poem and the need for the poet, as intercepting spirit, as go-between, to sift through the indiscriminate howls and yaps and to interpret or translate for us the significant messages masked in the noise of everyday life.

If this seems a slightly odd notion, it's because we're so accustomed to thinking of the artist as the origin or source of the art. The poet makes the poem, yes. The poet spills the words onto the page, one word behind another, and does so until the end of the line, and then until the end of another line, and so on until the poem is finished. The poet does, indeed, write the poem, but oddly enough, she does not create the impulse for the poem, the engendering idea, the imaginative seed, which is, arguably, the real creative act. I point here to the Irish poet Seamus Heaney, and to his notion of the two stages of the creative process, which he discusses in his essay "Feeling into Words." Stage one, what we might call the idea stage, he defines as that "first come-hither" of the poem, which presents itself as an image, a word, or perhaps even a phrase. This is followed, of course, by the making stage, the fleshing out of the poem onto the page. This making stage is clearly observable, but the idea stage is quite another story, much more mysterious and allusive, and therefore much more interesting.

As Mr. Warren, Mr. Heaney, and any number of poets

suggest, the seed of the poem, the idea, seems to come in some hazy way out of the world. Everyone, without exception, has experienced the excitement of "getting an idea." But who has ever stepped out of the shower, dried off, dressed, and walked into the kitchen to tell her spouse that she's just created a great idea? No, we say, rather, that we "got an idea" or "had an idea." All of this only echoes the great Mr. Yeats, who says in his autobiography, *The Trembling of the Veil:* "When a man writes any work of genius, or invents some creative action, is it not because some knowledge or power has come into his mind from beyond his mind?" Yes, this is to suggest that we experience this creative moment more as an act of reception, and that the creative moment is, indeed, a partially passive experience that is somewhat dependent on chance. If we are comfortable in accepting this description—and I am—then the question that arises immediately for the writer, or anyone who wants to facilitate the creative process, is this: When we all have access to essentially the same messages the world sends, why do some folks receive them readily and others hardly at all? Why can three people walk together across Woodruff Park in Atlanta and by the time they reach Peachtree Street only one get the idea for a poem? Why can three people walk down the same sidewalk, see the same squirrel carrying off a bag of Fritos, see the same homeless man asleep on a bench, the same businesswoman talking on a cell phone, and only one get the idea for a poem? From where does this gift of perception come? Seamus Heaney calls it a talent, a "gift for being in touch," by which he means an inborn predisposition to approach the world in a certain attentive way. In this sense, he says, the poet is a kind of "diviner," one who intuits signals from the world that others fail to detect. The metaphor he uses here is a water-dowser, a person who is able to divine with the use of a forked stick the presence of underground water. Heaney insists that this gift cannot be learned, but I like to think we all possess it to some degree and can hone whatever talent for divining we have. Indeed, like all other talents, without a great deal of exercise, it will most likely atrophy.

When I was a boy, as I mentioned, I listened to a lot of gospel music. One popular song I often heard on the radio was Albert Brumley's "Turn Your Radio On." One part goes like this, "Get a little taste of the joys awaiting. Get a little heaven in your soul, get in touch with God, turn your radio on." The implication here is that every soul, every spirit, is a radio receiver, a very apt metaphor for the poet, I think. Every soul is a radio receiver, but the poet has her radio turned on. The poet is, in the vernacular of my generation, "tuned-in." This heightened perception, this receptivity, is what Wordsworth in his famous preface to the *Lyrical Ballads* calls, a "more than usual organic sensibility." It is precisely that. The world sends signals constantly, millions in the time it takes to cross Peachtree Street or to find a seat at a Braves game or the symphony, but most of us tune in only what is immediately and obviously necessary to conduct our daily lives. This is the expedient way, since the greater part of everything else is background noise muddling the practical signals. And yet, as Robert Penn Warren suggests, the world is certainly trying to tell us more than whether the traffic light is green or red, or whether our box seat at the stadium is on the first- or third-base line. In that background noise there are messages about the connections in our lives, and the poet must not only have her radio turned on, she must be fine-tuned to those special suggestive signals, those subtle hints at the shadowy relationships that exist below the surface of things. And what are these signals, these clues to hidden meaning the world is constantly sending? Simply the metaphorical possibilities in everyday life, the suggestion of figurative connections.

Poetry more than any other literary genre rouses a language that rises above the literal and consequently evokes, as Ed Hirsch puts it, "a mode of *thinking* that moves beyond the literal." Yes, in poetry we actually begin to think in a different way, to open doors out of the physical landscape into an internal and spiritual landscape of more meaningful meanings and more truthful truths. To phrase this in a somewhat more mystical way, poetry is the literary genre that points most willingly to the veiled significance behind the physical world. These secrets unfold in the very unique relationship that poetry generates between reader and writer, an incredibly intimate relationship in which the interaction between individual minds depends largely on figurative expression. Few poets have been as heartened as I at the recent impulse toward narrative in American poetry, but I scratch my head at those poets who have pursued it almost single-mindedly at the expense of metaphor, which a legion of critics and poets from Aristotle to Richard Wilbur have identified, quite correctly, as the fundamental element of poetry.

Recently I spoke to a gathering of scientists and technicians at CIBA Vision in Atlanta. I was to talk with them about the subject of vision, which they certainly know something about, and having never spoken to a group of scientists before, I was slightly fearful that they might dismiss my notions of artistic vision as some wacky brand of transplanted California new-age hocus-pocus. They were, however, very receptive, and this experience sparked in me an interest in the unfortunate conflict that has developed in our culture between certain dogmatic advocates of science and the many folks who hold out for a more abundant and spirit-nurturing world view. I believe in science, don't get me wrong, and I'm very grateful for its many undeniable benefits, but I don't believe exclusively in science. Science covers well certain areas of our experience, but humans have needs to which science ministers poorly or cannot minister at all. I like the way the philosopher Huston Smith phrases this in his recent book *Why Religion Matters*:

> . . . the finitude of mundane existence cannot satisfy the human heart completely. Built into the human makeup is a longing for a "more" that the world of everyday experience cannot requite. This outreach strongly suggests the existence of the something that life reaches *for* in the way that the wings of birds point to the reality of air. Sunflowers bend in the direction of light because light exists . . .

I know this longing because I, too, feel it, and because the entire history of religion, art, and literature is a testament to it. Indeed, I think most artists will agree that there are many ways of knowing the world, and perhaps even the afterworld. "I am convinced," says Hirsch, "[that] the kind of experience—the kind of knowledge—one gets from poetry cannot be duplicated elsewhere." I don't hesitate to agree. Serious poetry is certainly an act of discovery, for the poet and the reader, and so a way of knowing. And what we discover through poetry, we discover through the power of the figurative. Story and physical detail are certainly important, but the poet never really creates anything physical in the poem. She only duplicates selected details of the original creation, only mimics and edits the first Creator. If there is any originality in the writing of a poem, it comes from the act of making metaphors, the act of giving new combinations to the various elements of the original creation. By harnessing two elements in a unique way, the poet can actually bring new dimension to both and at the same time imprint on the poem some sense of her own unique personality and world view. The gift of metaphor is simply the way it makes the world fresh, the way it teaches us to see the world from different angles, and the way it illustrates what Whitman calls "the vast similitude" that connects all things:

> All distances of place however wide,
> All distances of time, all inanimate forms,
> All souls, all living bodies though they be ever so
>   different, or in different worlds,
> All gaseous, watery, vegetable, mineral processes, the
>   fishes, the brutes,
> All nations, colors, barbarisms, civilizations, languages,
> All identities that have existed or may exist on this
>   globe, or any globe,
> All lives and deaths, all of the past, present, future . . .

Metaphor, indeed, is the connecting process, the

imaginative act of poetry that lets us leap beyond the confines of the physical world, beyond the confines of time and space.

So what does this say about the message of the poem? What does the poem tell us about the poet and what does it tell us about the reader? Or, perhaps, are the two messages really one in the same? I'm very attracted to Seamus Heaney's notion of the poem as personal archeology, the poem as personal dig. He says that the first time he ever wrote a poem he thought was truly good, he felt as though he'd "let down a shaft of light into himself." The poem can, indeed, be that sort of self-exploration, and quite often *is* to startling effect, but if the poem becomes meaningful in the largest sense, it will be an exploration of the personal that reveals the general contours of human experience. It will be a process that begins with the one but reveals the many. It will illustrate the large connection, "the vast similitude." As Jane Hirshfield says in her essay "The Question of Originality": "We turn to Shakespeare's sonnets to learn not about Shakespeare's life but about our own. The beauty, feeling, and understanding they hold throw off a continuing brightness, and within its circle the hand holding the page is also freshly lit." Yes, we as readers are that self-centered, and the poem that means in the fullest way will discover in the personal a connection to the whole. In fact, all serious poems start with the premise that the experience of the poet is not hers alone, but is in a vital way representative of every person on the planet. And herein, of course, lies the contagious power of poetry, which is simply the blessing of newfound significance. A small enlightenment begins to burn in one person and before long the effect is seen in a neighborhood, a community, a culture.

One of my favorite movies illustrates this well. In his

1995 movie *Il Postino*, director Michael Radford tells the story of a small Italian island awakened to a higher consciousness by a visit from the exiled Chilean poet Pablo Neruda. The story is told through the eyes of Mario Ruoppolo, a postman who delivers Neruda's mail. Like most of the people on the island, Mario is very poor and without prospects. The islanders subsist, and barely that, on fishing. Mario hates fishing, and he lives under a cloud of deprivation and hopelessness. He is, however, not illiterate like many of his neighbors. Though uneducated, he can read and write, and when he comes across a book of Neruda's poems, he becomes curious about and then enamored of this man of ideas, this poet who sees in the various elements of the world beauties and possibilities that he and his neighbors have overlooked. One of my favorite lines in the movie comes when Mario falls in love with Beatrice, a beautiful young woman who works in her aunt's hotel and tavern. Mario is deeply smitten but he cannot communicate his feelings to this woman. He fumbles, stammers, turns mute every time he tries to speak to her. His spirit needs to find a voice, his spirit wants articulation. He needs not just words, but appropriate words, compelling words, words that are worthy of his emotion—so he sends her a poem, a poem he plagiarizes from Neruda's book. Beatrice is at first puzzled. She reads the poem, she reads it again. Gradually the images take hold, and the poem works its magic. Gradually she is swept away by Neruda's language and her world is changed. So much so that she notices Mario Ruoppolo. So much so that her aunt, much dismayed, notices her noticing Mario Ruoppo, and when her aunt discovers the poem, she takes it to Neruda to complain that her niece is being seduced.

Seduced by metaphors, corrupted by metaphors!

This sets up the most illuminating line in the movie. When Neruda confronts Mario, very sympathetically, about his failure to confess his love and about stealing his poem, Mario says, "Poetry doesn't belong to those who write it, but to those who need it." I love that. There's something powerfully revealing in the desperation of that statement. "Poetry doesn't belong to those who write it, but to those who need it."

Poetry, we must understand, not only fills a personal need, but a cultural need as well, and *Il Postino* is a narrow but vivid glimpse into the way poetry enhances the spiritual health of a community. Neruda's poetry not only works its medicine on Mario and Beatrice, but gradually on Beatrice's aunt and a few other members of the community. Even the islanders who are not directly touched by the power of Neruda's language recognize the presence in their lives of a new and intangible significance. A fresh and powerful force has been loosed on their community, and it has changed the lives of a few of their neighbors. Out of the new ways these few folks approach the world, the island as a whole gradually rises to a higher level of awareness, to a greater appreciation of the natural beauties around them, and to a greater sense of significance in their lives and their traditions. So it is, I'll wager, with all poetry and all cultures.

My subject here has been the poem, but I've been talking, of course, about all arts, all creative endeavors that seek out the ultimate meaning of our lives. Speaking of his life as a writer, Dickey once wrote: "It seems to me that I am the bearer of some kind of immortal message to humankind. What is this message? I don't know, but it exists." Of course, he did know, although he chooses here to leave the question hanging. The message is the message of all poets and all poems at all times. It's the announcement of our commonality, our fundamental humanity, the significance of being the human creature at our particular moment in the world. It is a reminder to stay focused, to stay tuned-in, to continue the endless struggle of putting ourselves in the proper relationship with the enduring mysteries.

I want to close with a poem that may suggest some, or all, or perhaps none of the points I've tried to make, the title poem of my third book. Back in the early eighties I attended Florida State University in Tallahassee, where I received my Ph.D. in bass fishing. I had a little aluminum boat and a small outboard motor, and I liked to cruise up and down the little rivers around Tallahassee, dragging a wad of dead worms behind me. One of my favorite rivers, I remember, was the Wakulla, though I don't think I ever actually caught a fish out of those waters. Still, it was a gorgeous place. You'll know something of what I'm saying if I tell you that back in the early forties two of those Johnny Weissmuller Tarzan movies were made there, along with a movie called *The Creature from the Black Lagoon*. It was jungle, or about as close to jungle as one could get in the Florida panhandle.

Anyway, I was out in my boat one morning, just after daybreak, I think, when I came into a bend of the river, and about halfway through that bend a clearing opened up on the far bank. In the middle of this clearing stood one giant tree, jet black. It looked very strange and gave me an odd feeling—it looked as though someone had taken a piece of black construction paper and cut out the silhouette of a giant oak tree and pasted it there on the bank. Then the feeling turned stranger because I could see that the tree was speckled all over with pink fruit. It was some sort of gigantic weird fruit tree. I drifted a little closer then and felt really odd because I saw that these things were not fruit at all. They were heads, and they were the heads of vultures. I'd come on a buzzard roost, the first I'd ever seen. And they were packed into that tree literally shoulder to shoulder, so thick I could hardly see light through it.

Several years later, I was doing some reading about vultures, about how they are actually revered in other cultures, and I remembered that tree. A line or a phrase came to me, and I suddenly saw those vultures in a different way. Somewhere in the depths of my psyche a transformation had taken place, a re-evaluation of the American buzzard, and out of that came a poem called "Under the Vulture-Tree":

Under the Vulture-Tree

We have all seen them circling pastures,
have looked up from the mouth of a barn, a pine clearing,
the fences of our own backyards, and have stood
amazed by the one slow wing beat, the endless dihedral drift.
But I had never seen so many so close, hundreds,
every limb of the dead oak feathered black,

and I cut the engine, let the river grab the jon boat
and pull it toward the tree.
The black leaves shined, the pink fruit blossomed
red, ugly as a human heart.
Then, as I passed under their dream, I saw for the first time
its soft countenance, the raw fleshy jowls
wrinkled and generous, like the faces of the very old
who have grown to empathize with everything.

And I drifted away from them, slow, on the pull of the river,

reluctant, looking back at their roost,
calling them what I'd never called them, what they are,
those dwarfed transfiguring angels,
who flock to the side of the poisoned fox, the mud turtle
crushed on the shoulder of the road,
who pray over the leaf-graves of the anonymous lost,
with mercy enough to consume us all and give us wings.

THIRST AND THE WRITER'S SENSE
OF CONSEQUENCE

A few weeks ago while thumbing through a new anthology, I ran across a little poem I hadn't seen in years. It's a well-known poem by Walt Whitman called "A Noiseless Patient Spider":

> A noiseless patient spider,
> I mark'd where on a little promontory it stood isolated,
> Mark'd how to explore the vacant vast surrounding,
> It launch'd forth filament, filament, filament, out of itself,
> Ever unreeling them, ever tirelessly speeding them.
>
> And you O my soul where you stand,
> Surrounded, detached, in measureless oceans of space,
> Ceaselessly musing, venturing, throwing, seeking the spheres to connect
>   them,
> Till the bridge you will need be form'd, till the ductile anchor hold,
> Till the gossamer thread you fling catch somewhere, O my soul.

I had always admired the beautiful way this poem catches the human need to connect, to empathize and to find empathy, to love and be loved, and the way it suggests the writer's role as an explorer of the unknown, who seeks "the spheres to connect them," who seeks the mysteries to tie them all together. But what surprised me and intrigued me on this re-reading was its urgency of longing and the sweep of its immeasurable range. Once again I started to ponder the whole question of artistic sensibility, more specifically, the sensibility that gives impulse to poetry and literary fiction. What I'm talking about is the characteristic of personality that makes a writer seek serious expression through language, the impulse that makes the soul launch forth "filament, filament, filament, out of itself." Robert Penn Warren suggested that this impulse was, in his case, the quality of spiritual yearning. "I am a creature of this world," he told *The Gettysburg Review* editor Peter Stitt in a 1977 interview, "but I am also a yearner, I suppose." Though he had no theology, he said, the world seemed to him infused with hidden spiritual significance, and he yearned for verification of this.

I'm attracted to this notion of yearning, this longing, what the poet Charles Wright calls "a thirst," because it echoes strongly in many of my earliest memories of reading. Two come immediately to mind. In the first I'm in the seventh or eighth grade, sitting in our living room in Canton, Georgia, prowling through a story by Edgar Allan Poe. I believe this was my first encounter with the ill-omened spirit of the Lady Ligeia and her efforts to find bodily re-entry into this world, but that part of the memory has faded. What's left is only the feel of our sofa, a halo of yellow light struggling through a lampshade, and most importantly, a still powerful sense of pursuit, of quest, of anticipation of discovery pulsing through me.

Another memory in which this feeling is especially intense is of an evening a year or so later. I'm sitting in our living room, on that same couch, in the yellow light of that same lamp, reading in the *Collected Poems* of W. B. Yeats, which I've checked out of the county library. I'm baffled, but caught, helpless. A few puzzling images have dug in like hooks—a fly with long legs moving over silent water, the sleepy soldiers of some Emperor, a creature with the body of a lion and the head of a man. Of course, I understood little or nothing of Yeats' meanings. However, I sensed deeply the anticipation, the desire to discover, that prompted me to dig into those mysterious poems and plow, as best as I could, through their strange sounds and imagery.

That anticipation, which I still experience occasionally when reading, is certainly why I fell in love with stories and poems and ultimately, no doubt, with the notion of trying to write them. It was a sense of anticipation, which I had come to associate exclusively with books. I remember the way it flowed through me as I flipped the pages, looking for an interesting title, a promising poem. Though I would not have been able to name it then, I understand it now as a feeling of consequence. Something about Yeats' poems seemed significant in purpose. Something about those poems felt as though they might point me in the direction of consequence in the world, and perhaps, in another world. Those poems seemed to be on the trail of something, an answer to a question I carried inside myself, a sense of significance deeper than my individual life, a meaning for which, in Warren's sense, I seemed to be yearning.

* * *

I try to teach writing, and I try to write, so occasionally I think about the creative process and the mission and offices of the writer. Most folks these days who are interested in teaching the craft of poems, stories, and novels are in the business of demystifying the writing process and the role of the writer in the world. Evidence of this abounds in the enormous stack of practical writing guides that have been published over the past few years—books that tell us everything we'd ever want to know about the particulars of syntax, character development, symbolism, or figurative language—but tell us little or nothing about the creative process itself. Never, in fact, have I seen the authors of any these guides even attempt to talk about the nature of the creative urge and how that might define the relationship between the writer and the world. This is perilous territory, true, where one must step cautiously along the borders of psychology and mysticism, and conversation here has become difficult because such discussions require broad statements that are ultimately insupportable, a misdemeanor, at least, in a scientific and secular culture such as ours.

A case in point. A few months ago I was talking to a group of young poets and our conversation bounced from questions about the creative process and the origins of ideas to the existence and nature of a divine creator. I asked them then to think for a moment and silently to categorize themselves as: 1) a believer in a divine and purposeful creator, 2) an agnostic, in the sense of someone who doubts but holds opens the possibility of a divine and purposeful creator, or 3) a complete non-believer in all that otherworldly business. A general embarrassment broke out, and after a few seconds I said, "Okay, if you find yourself among the first two groups, you may have a chance of becoming a serious poet. If you count yourself among the latter, you're chances may be diminished." The embarrassment in the room turned into a profound discomfort. Some people were clearly angry. One fellow took out a small but ominous-looking pocket knife and began cleaning his nails. He gave me a very bad look.

The totally insupportable thing that I said to those young poets and want to repeat now is that the greatest writers, the writers who touch their readers at the deepest emotional and psychological levels, are most frequently those poets and story-tellers who are yearners after meaning. They use their art, as Yeats said in a 1918 letter to Ezra Pound, "as their tool of investigation." Indeed, I'm inclined to say that this brand of yearning is, indeed, the characteristic that gives impulse to all great poetry, and perhaps all profound art and science. It's the simple but insistent longing to discover significance in the world, the need to understand not only how the world works, but why. We usually associate this sort of desire with science and philosophy, but that doesn't mean it's any less prevalent in art. The creative urge itself indicates a hunger for order and purpose in a world that only grudgingly gives up any evidence of such. Should it surprise us then that the writers who affect readers most deeply are those poets and story-tellers who have not abandoned hope for the possibility of the human soul? What the die-hard atheist gives up, but what the believer and the agnostic may share, is that sense of hope, that yearning to discover some ultimate purpose in one's life and in the world. Flannery O'Connor suggests a similar notion in her essay "Novelist and Believer." Here she writes:

> The novelist doesn't write about people in a vacuum; he writes about people in a world where something is obviously lacking, where there is the general mystery of incompleteness . . . , and the novelist tries to give you, within the form of the book, a total experience of human nature at any time. For this reason the greatest dramas naturally involve the salvation or loss of the soul. Where there is no belief in the soul, there is very little drama.

True enough. Where there is no belief in the soul, or no belief in the possibility of the soul, there is, truly, very little at stake. Significance never stretches far beyond our present moment in history—what we did yesterday, what we expect to do tomorrow or the next, all a series of events moving inevitably toward one conclusion. And for the writer who abandons hope for the soul, even the writer who is grateful for life in the present moment, the voice can turn too easily to lamentation and cynicism.

Though testing O'Connor's notion against the canon of world literature is something slightly beyond the scope of my expertise, I feel fairly safe in asserting that the eternal is always more significant than the temporal. Still, many of us will probably be tempted to run this notion through a few of our favorite books. After I came across that passage in O'Connor's essay, I immediately thought of a handful of my own favorite novels. Two are by Dostoevsky, *The Brothers Karamazov* and *Crime and Punishment,* and following closely comes Hawthorne's *The Scarlet Letter* and Melville's *Moby-Dick*. Every few years I read these books again, and I think now that what continues to draw me to these novels, and what seems to link them to other great novels, is the profound religious sensibility that pervades them. In each story this sensibility is a dramatically crucial, indeed defining, attribute. For instance, imagine *The Brothers Karamazov* absent Alyosha's concern for Dmitri's soul or Ivan's agonizing "The Grand Inquistor," or imagine The *Scarlet Letter* without the religious consequences of Dimmesdale and Hester's adultery. In *Moby-Dick* this sensibility expresses itself more symbolically, but it's still a powerful and dominant presence in the quest for the white whale. Without these spiritual dimensions we'd have only a few pretty good adventure stories. This, indeed, is the very characteristic in Flannery O'Connor's fiction that links her more closely to these great novelists than to fellow writers of the modern Southern gothic, with whom she is often grouped. For instance, if we remove the Catholic foundation from O'Connor's work, what we have left is the grotesque and one-dimensional fiction of Erskine Caldwell or Harry Crews.

* * *

I'm not trying to say that every good writer is a religious person. I am suggesting, though, that the greatest writers seem to be those folks who exhibit a religious sensibility, at least in the sense of probing the profound questions of the human predicament. This is difficult for us these days. We live in the age of reason. Our ruling myth is science, and we have real difficulty trusting anything beyond the measurable physical world. Carl Jung, in his wonderful little book

Modern Man in Search of a Soul, tells us that we blind ourselves "to our religious promptings because of a childish passion for rational enlightenment," and this often causes us serious psychic harm. One doesn't have to look far to find overwhelming evidence of this, on both the personal and cultural levels. We have lost touch not only with the mysteries of the natural creation, which we continue to devalue, but with the mysteries of our own being, our own inner life.

Again, I'm not suggesting that every good writer is a devoutly religious person, only that the greatest writers seem to exhibit a clearly discernable religious sensibility. Of his own experience, Warren said in that same interview with Stitt, "I would call this temperament rather than theology . . . that is, I feel an immanence of meaning in things, but I have no meaning to put there that is interesting or beautiful. I think I put it as close as I could in a poem called "Masts at Dawn"—We must try/To love so well the world that we may believe, in the end, in God."

I've always loved that line because it points beautifully to the writer's proper approach toward the world, which is always through a sense of awe. "We must try," Warren says, which is sufficient witness to that condition of yearning, that state of longing. We desire meaning in our lives—we yearn for significance—therefore we must try to find it in the objects and actions of the world. This is, for Warren, the charge of the writer—to be an explorer, a searcher, a seeker of the ultimate. His starting point, and ours, is the physical world, but his goal is the revelation of meaning behind the operations of the world. As he says in a fine poem about his parents, "I Am Dreaming of a White Christmas: The Natural History of a Vision":

All items listed above belong in the world
In which all things are continuous,
And are parts of the original dream which
I am now trying to discover the logic of.

We, of course, did not dream "the original dream," and, being inside the dream, we are incapable of comprehending its total meaning. Still, glimpses of that meaning suggest themselves to us at various moments in our lives, and the possibility of puzzling those glimpses into a complete picture eats at us constantly.

* * *

I remember James Dickey sitting at my dining room table one morning back in the mid-eighties. We'd gotten up late and had skipped breakfast, so we'd raided the fridge for what was left of a Honey-baked ham. I don't remember what we'd been talking about, but Dickey was picking at the ham with his fingers and doing a fine job of finishing it off, when he glared at me across the table. He took one of his long thoughtful breaths and bared his teeth. "You know," he said, "sometimes I think I can almost see right through it, right through it all, right to the bone."

He wasn't talking about ham, of course, but about those rare and teasing moments of clarity when we think that we might see right into the absolute core of things. He'd experienced moments of clarity so intense, he said, that he felt if he could just tie them all together, just draw a line between them in the way one might connect the dots of a puzzle, he would have an outline of the true story. (His version, I suppose, of Whitman's soul as spider "seeking the spheres to connect them.") James Joyce, of course, called these moments of clarity "epiphanies," a religious word he secularized to refer to a deep insight. Wordsworth called them "spots of time." Out of these moments, good writers, when lucky, make good poems and stories, and so each poem or story is, in its own way, a dot in Dickey's puzzle. The poet or the fiction writer who wants to touch readers on the deepest level is constantly seeking out those dots and trying to connect them, acting against desperate odds on the impulse of yearning to know. In this way, literature becomes a record of the ways the world moves us toward a sense of significance. The world is constantly trying to tell the poet something, Warren liked to suggest. But the world is coy. It will not explain itself outright. Its strategies are the strategies of the poem. Its language is imagery, its method innuendo. It teases us, lures us, prods us toward discovery, and if we are to learn what it has to reveal, we must accept the challenge of the quest. Listen to these well-known lines from the concluding section of "Aubudon: A Vision," lines that describe Warren's first waking up to the mysteries of the world:

> Long ago in Kentucky, I, a boy, stood
> By a dirt road, in first dark, and heard
> The great geese hoot northward.
> I could not see them, there being no moon
> And the stars sparse. I heard them.
>
> I did not know what was happening in my heart.
>
> It was the season before the elderberry blooms,
> Therefore they were going north.
>
> The sound was passing northward.

A boy stands on a dirt road, at night, alone. The geese pass overhead, unseen in the darkness. Yet he hears them. They are a real, if invisible, part of the world, a small but real component of the world's mystery. He hears, in short, a moving element in the processes of nature, and something primal stirs inside him. The world has stirred a longing, has issued a call, unmistakable in its presence, but hazy in its particulars. Even years later he can only say, "I did not know what was happening in my heart."

* * *

Art as quest for truth, for ultimate reality, is a notion that has always appealed to me. Not always, though, does the yearning for meaning focus its search on the exterior world. Reality, as we all know, is not exclusively external. We, in short, have an inner life. One powerful irony of art is that while it moves outward into the world, it may be moving simultaneously inward, into the realm of the unconscious psyche, that murky reservoir of image, fear, and desire, which mirrors in darker ways the subtle and often hidden truths of the natural world.

One of my first glimpses into the frightening possibilities of the inner life, the frightening power of the imagination and the dream, came in my childhood and twenty or so years later spun itself into a poem called "Appearances." When I was eight or nine years old, I heard on a radio news report that a UFO had been sighted in a field in south Georgia. There had been several UFO reports that summer, and I was both curious and alarmed by them. This report, however, seemed particularly disturbing because the "craft," the "thing," or whatever it was, appeared to have something liquid inside it. I'd never put much stock in little green men, which seemed entirely too anthropomorphic, not really alien enough to be real, but a living liquid seemed entirely alien, bizarre, frightening, and credible. Therein, lay my great horror. In the poem the sheriff's deputies search the field and discover that the object of terror and intrigue is actually a broken piece of a neon sign. However, this discovery, the poem says, "is nothing to ease my sleep":

> I dream of the whole universe, of an infinite
> and indiscriminate creation
>
> where the black frontier behind the eyes floats back as far
>
> as the light behind the stars.

The yearner knows that the "black frontier behind the eyes," the inner life of the psyche, is a land of treasure and hidden powers, but also a land of perils. It is, in short, a land of magic, both good and bad, and going there often requires some courage. It is in the deepest sense the underworld, and there are secrets in that world we'd rather not encounter. "The dread and the resistance," Jung tells us, "which every natural human being experiences when it comes to delving too deeply into himself is, at bottom, the fear of Hades." But the writer who is also a seeker must learn to move by faith across that dangerous terrain, to trust in his or her own hidden strengths, to nourish them, to apply them in artful ways in our search for meaning. This amounts to nothing less than giving ourselves up to the uninhibited contents of the unconscious as they manifest themselves in myth, fairy-tale, trance, and dream.

Edward Hirsch finds a wonderful metaphor for this in the act of sleepwalking. Listen to a few lines from his poem "For the Sleepwalkers":

> I love the way that sleepwalkers are willing
> to step out of their bodies into the night,
> to raise their arms and welcome the darkness,
>
> palming the blank spaces, touching everything.
> Always they return home safely, like blind men
> who know it is morning by feeling shadows.
>
> . . . . .
>
> We have to learn to trust our hearts like that.
> We have to learn the desperate faith of sleep-
> walkers who rise out of their calm beds
>
> and walk through the skin of another life.
> We have to drink the stupefying cup of darkness
> and wake up to ourselves, nourished and surprised.

* * *

So, how do these observations about yearning for meaning, assuming they're true, affect our lives as writers and readers? Specifics are elusive here, because many effects will, no doubt be personal. Perhaps, though, in some way our awareness of our roles as yearners may help us hone our stance toward the world, our way of perceiving, our way of catching the messages, the clues, the hints the world sends. A searcher certainly watches and listens with a heightened intensity, a yearner certainly moves through the world with a greater sense of urgency. Gradually then, all things of this world intensify as they become vehicles for the possibility of consequence. Also, this awareness may teach us not to close down possibilities, not to close ourselves off from the difficult or the improbable. It couldn't hurt to take Warren's charge as our own. "We must try," he writes, "To so well love the world that we may believe, in the end, in God," which is to say that we must avidly pursue our role as yearner and seeker, that we must hold out hope for the soul, hold out hope for the possibility of meaning and purpose in a world that grudgingly suggests such. "I have a thirst for the divine," says poet Charles Wright, "a long drink of forbidden water./ I have a hankering for the dust-light, for all thing illegible" ("Lost Language"). Flannery O'Connor would certainly agree. Only that thirst, that impulse, that hope, can give birth to a story or a poem of the deepest significance.

WHAT THE GRAVEYARD SAYS:
A THOUGHT ON THE
CONSEQUENCE OF PLACE

There are those for whom place is unimportant,"
says Theodore Roethke in his wonderful poem
"The Rose." I have never been one of those people.
As a writer who lived his entire childhood on one small
plot of family-invested ground, place for me has always been
of utmost significance. This, however, may be less a matter
of geography or history than a matter of sensibility. But I
should probably clarify at the outset my particular focus, the
sort of place I mean to talk about. I'm not expressly concerned
here with the region a writer inhabits and comes to call
home, the place that seeps into personality and gradually
influences his or her stance in approaching the outside
world—say the Montana of Richard Hugo or the Alaska of
John Haines, or more specifically, the Kentucky farm of
Wendell Berry. Such places of long habitation certainly work
crucial influences on a writer's art, but I'm more concerned
with what I might call spots, those more particular places,
within or not the communities we call home, that speak to us

in strong ways when we encounter them. These are essentially spots that serve less as developers of sensibility and more as catalysts for specific poems. They attract and spark, I believe, a sensibility that is already active.

For me poetry has always started with a sense of the mysteries, with a hazy intuition of a reality other than the physical world. Early on—and I'm speaking here of my undergraduate years at Mercer—this was a direction I picked up through imitation. I felt it in the work of my favorite poets, writers who practiced poetry as an act of discovery, who used language to explore the world's perceived secrets. Though I wouldn't have been able to articulate it, this was the quality I loved in several early Romantics, especially Blake, Wordsworth, and Coleridge. I thought I found the same thing in the sonorous obscurities of Dylan Thomas, and did find it later in the myth and mysticism of Yeats and in the nature poetry of Theodore Roethke. It was poetry used for what Wordsworth calls seeing "into the life of things." It was the poetry of the seeker, the searcher after significance, who studies, as Roethke says, "the lives on a leaf" and finds years later that "All finite things reveal infinitude." I don't know that I ever attempted to articulate this approach to poetry, or thought much about it, until Robert Penn Warren said it for me in an introduction he wrote for the Library of Congress in 1985. Speaking of my first two books but describing more accurately his own vision, he said, "Underlying all his work is the simple and unusual conviction that the world we see is trying to tell us something." This still seems a cogent comment on the way the poets I admire have approached their art. What the world ultimately reveals to the poet in its many secret messages are the metaphorical possibilities in our everyday lives, and the sum of these communications suggests a consequence, a sense of purpose underlying the imagery of the physical world. Ultimately the poem itself seeks to make language work metaphorically in order to reproduce, explore, and memorialize this process of the world. As Warren says in his fine poem "I Am Dreaming of a White Christmas: The Natural History of a Vision":

> All items listed above belong in the world
> In which all things are continuous,
> And are parts of the original dream which
> I am now trying to discover the logic of.

Roethke, in one of his notebooks, calls for just such a poetry: "A poetry of longing: not for escape, but for a greater reality." This is a poetry that demands of language the same investigative function that Seamus Heaney implies in his well-known metaphor of "digging." Yeats suggests it metaphorically in a number of poems, but says it outright in a 1918 letter to Ezra Pound. "After all," he writes, "one's art is not the chief end of life but an accident in one's search for reality or rather perhaps one's method of search."

Not every poet, of course, shares such a vision, and I don't mean to call any other approach wrongheaded. I am speaking merely of my own notions of language as art and how I came by them. I certainly don't assume them to be universal, or even common. To be a seeker may be, indeed, as Warren says, to be "unusual." In fact, one might even say to be eccentric, antiquated, a soft-headed dealer in the arcane. To be a seeker requires, at the very least, a belief in the possibility of what Roethke calls "a greater reality" and what Warren calls "the original dream." Indeed, in this age of scientism it may require something of a rational wobble, an inability to walk a straight and logical line. The seeker is, truly, always a little bit off kilter, always a little puzzled, always searching for the stable unchanging answer. If I had to name this quality in a writer, I would simply call it a "religious sensibility"—not a religion, of course, but a particular sort of receptivity, a receptivity profoundly attracted to the possibility of other realities veiled in the images of our everyday lives. I'm simply talking about a trait that holds at its core an intuitive gift to supplement the findings of the five senses. This religious sensibility, this notion of poet as "seeker," which I take from all of the poets mentioned above and many others, explains to some degree why certain landscapes and spots in and around Macon have compelled my imagination toward poetry.

* * *

Thirty-three years have passed since I lived in Macon, Georgia. Still, in every book I've published I've touched on a Macon landscape. It takes no great insight to conclude that Macon and its surroundings have exerted a strong influence on my imagination. One reason for this may be the fact that my five years spent here came at the beginning of my adulthood and spanned my first efforts at writing poetry. They were, as folks like to say at commencement exercises, those formative years of idealism and endless possibility. That, however, will not serve entirely. In mulling over these years again, I'm convinced that certain characteristics of the place itself were significant, and that other places I've lived would not have moved me in the same direction or propelled me with the same force.

Macon is the first place I ever lived that exuded a significant sense of history. If such a statement sounds odd, remember that I was born and raised in Canton, Georgia, a very small town in which everything of any cultural or historical value was, over the years, systematically bulldozed for the quick bucks of burger joints and car washes. Macon suggested, at least, a sense of a cultural past, and I don't twist the truth far out of shape when I say that the ante-bellum homes along College Street seemed to me on first sight like something out of *Gone With the Wind*. Very soon I discovered the Cannon Ball House on Mulberry Street, and pondered its small part in the Civil War. And close by stood the Hay House. There were rumors that it had once housed secret Confederate gold and that an underground tunnel ran from its cellar all the way to the river, in case the Rebels had to move that gold quickly. I was also interested in the Sidney Lanier cottage. A real poet had been born here. Never mind that I'd never actually read any of his poems. I felt some sense of consequence that the town in which I was living had nurtured at least one writer. Although the house was still a private residence when I was a student at Mercer, I visited it several times in the mid-seventies, shortly after it opened to the public, to see for myself what evidence it provided of a real life—a few paintings, editions of his books, his wife's wedding dress. And locked away in a bookcase, his alto flute, his alligator slippers, a copy of the only book of poems he published during his lifetime. Once the lady who managed the place, opened the case and let me hold that book. When she turned her head for a second, I pressed a key on his flute and rubbed the toe of a slipper.

Other places seem on first glance to be much less poetic. One of these was the Sunshine Club on Forsyth Street, a tiny beer joint that catered to frat boys and later to local rednecks and hard-core bikers. In a poem from my first book I wrote of it, "All night long I've been sitting in this booth, watching beehives and tight skirts,/gold earrings glowing and fading in the turning light of a Pabst Blue Ribbon sign," which seems now to be largely fantasy, since the only woman I actually remember seeing at the Sunshine Club caused a bar fight that soured me on the place for a good long while.

Macon, however, did have its fair share of joints awash in "beehives and tight skirts." Cotton Avenue had Betty's Lounge, and Cherry Street had Ruby's Brass Rail. Broadway had Anne's Tic-Toc and Lee's Lounge, where on weekends you could dance to good Western swing, that is, if you happened to be appareled in shoes and a shirt. These places held for me a curious fascination, a fascination that I can explain only as my redneck equivalent to Wordsworth's interest in "low and rustic life," as he tags it in his 1802 preface to the *Lyrical Ballads*. At the Sunshine, Lee's Lounge, or Ruby's Brass Rail, I could observe, I thought, human nature at its most natural, free of the corruptions and inhibitions of proper Southern society, especially when it danced on the waves of a few tall Budweisers.

Many other places, public and private, worked on my imagination—the Ocmulgee Indian mounds, a haunted house on Bond Street, the Bibb County dump. The point hones down to this. I found in Macon a number of spots where I felt a sense of consequence. Each of these places seemed capable of revealing something of "the real life," as Wordsworth calls it, and first among these was Rose Hill Cemetery.

* * *

I'm very attracted to Warren's notion about the world trying to tell the poet something, and I try to go about my life keeping my receptors tuned for whatever might come. One would think, though, that a cemetery might speak rather clearly, and bluntly, and that no one would have to listen very closely to catch its meaning. On the rational level this is true enough—the message of the graveyard is unambiguous. But to that other part of ourselves, the part that houses the "yearner," the graveyard insinuates a number of other messages.

I discovered Rose Hill shortly after I arrived in Macon in the fall of 1968. My first trips into the cemetery were stone-rubbing excursions with my girlfriend, an art major at Wesleyan, who was interested in tombstone art. She loved to do charcoal and rice-paper rubbings of old gravestones, and I loved to wander around the hills, reading the epitaphs, which were sometimes fairly startling. One of my favorites reads: "She's Gone! Forever Gone! The King of Terrors/ Lays His Rude Hands Upon Her Lovely Limbs,/And Blasts Her Beauties With His Icy Breath"—curious lines from John Dennis' entirely obscure 18th century treatment of "Appius and Virginia," and a little more horror, a little more anger, than I was accustomed to seeing expressed in grief. Still, this didn't seem out of place in Rose Hill. I'd really never seen such a graveyard, the kind that inspires movie sets—elaborate Victorian statuary, marble mausoleums, and the plain stone markers of the Confederate dead, all set into a landscape of tree-shaded hills. There were gothic brick crypts dug into a hillside, and across the valley, behind a huge wallow of undergrowth, an actual open grave gapped in the side of a ridge. The Ocmulgee River provided another symbolic layer. All of these things combined to work a vigorous influence. Sometimes it seemed that I could sense a palpable presence drifting among those stones. It was more, I think, than the feeling of memorialized history, more than a vague sense of anonymous lives gone before and lost, suggesting what also waited for me. In short, I found there what a few people still find in old graveyards. I found a haunted place, and Rose Hill became for me a landscape on which to ponder what Warren called the logic of "the original dream."

Several early poems came out of that graveyard, but the first that was competent enough to publish was called "Smoking in an Open Grave." It came to me around 1977 and found its way into a little magazine called *New Letters* and a while later into a poetry handbook edited by X.J. Kennedy. The poem deals with that empty tomb cut into the north ridge of Lakeside Terrace, and it echoes a standard theme of burial and rebirth. I remember, though, being very interested then in the ritual of burial—certainly tied to my experience with gravestone rubbings—and I was also very taken with Joseph Campbell's *Primitive Mythology,* which was likely my first experience with myth. At any rate, in the poem the persona and a few friends crawl into that open grave to smoke marijuana, play guitars, and sing old spirituals. "We bury ourselves to get high," he says, and though the poem struggles for some originality in the irony of the pun, the sentiment remains fairly conventional, a rehash of the English graveyard school, to which X.J. Kennedy linked it. What I still find interesting, though, is the strategy of that quest. The persona, looking for ultimate answers, has gone more or less instinctively into a graveyard. In English poetry the first step down this path may have been taken around 1722, when Thomas Parnell wrote a poem called "A Night Piece on Death," a forerunner of Gray's famous elegy. Seeking wisdom, Parnell abandons scholars and books and visits a truer teacher, a country graveyard, where he discovers that "Death's but a path that must be trod/If man would ever pass to God."

Conventional as my poem might seem, that open grave was truly exotic. Bizarre, indeed, is not too strong a word, and I remember thinking on one of my first visits that if Yeats had lived in Macon, he certainly would have found his way to it and written it into the ceremonies of The Golden Dawn. Mercer's first bonafide hippy, Thomas Michael, showed me this grave early on in my explorations of Rose Hill. Apparently the spot wasn't well-known. Chuck Leavell told me recently that when he was with the Allman Brothers Band in the early seventies, he spent some serious time in Rose Hill and never ran across it. At that time, though, the valley in front of the grave was overgrown, and the grave lay hidden behind a dense thicket. It wasn't easy to reach. What you found, however, if you persisted, was the open mouth of a tomb, with "stubs of iron bars/jagging those jaws like rusty teeth," as I described it years later in a poem called "The Resurrection." In order to crawl in, you had to get down on your hands and knees. A narrow passage opened then, something like an igloo, into a domed earthen room maybe ten or twelve feet across. I remember broken beer bottles, whiskey bottles, some scratching on the walls, that's about it. But all of this made for some very romantic stories. The best was a rumor that this was the meeting place of a local witches' coven. About this, I know nothing, and over the years I've been unable to find out anything at all about that grave. Apparently the body or bodies were exhumed a good long time ago and the grave left empty.

In my poem "The Resurrection," which was written in the early eighties, the grave is used by a man and a woman for a sexual rendezvous, but a framework of Christian imagery supports the poem. And how could it not, given the nature of the place? One goes into a place like that and comes out a new person, or so the pattern goes. I used this spot in a similar way a few years later in a novel called *Easter Weekend* in which the protagonist, Connie Holtzclaw, steals a large wad of money from some Macon thugs and hides out in this grave on the night before Easter. Connie's fate at the end of the book is ambiguous, which is a statement, I suppose, about the whole notion of burial, rebirth, and the function of faith.

* * *

When I was an undergraduate at Mercer, Rose Hill was in a general state of neglect, but for me this only added an extra layer of romance. In fact, the decay of the cemetery seemed as suggestive as the stones and crypts themselves. Many plots were overgrown, and vandalism was not uncommon—angels had broken arms and wings, stones were broken or overturned. Years later when thinking about Rose Hill this is what I remembered, and the vandalism seemed to me then a crude sort of rebellion against the whole notion of a graveyard and the indisputable fact that necessitated it. As I thought about that I began to put myself into the mind of one of those vandals. I began to imagine going through the cemetery with a crowbar and a drag chain to break up angels and stones. What I was after, of course, was motive. Why would anyone commit such a disgraceful act? What was to be gained from this sort of destruction? Out of that came a less conventional poem called "Wrestling Angels":

> With crowbars and drag chains
> we walk tonight through a valley of tombs
> where the only sounds are frogs in the reeds
> and the river whispering at the foot of Rose Hill
> that we have come to salvage from the dead.
>
> Only the ironwork will bring us money,
> ornamental sofas overlooking graves,
> black-flowered fences planted in marble,
> occasionally an urn or a bronze star.
>
> But if there is time
> we shatter the hourglasses,
> slaughter lambs asleep on children's graves,
> break the blades off stone scythes,
> the marble strings on silent lyres.
> Only the angels are hear to stop us, and they have grown
> too weak to wrestle.
> We break their arms and leave them wingless,
> leaning over graves like old men lamenting their age.

If the persona offers "ironwork" or whatever can be salvaged and sold as a motive for his vandalism, we discover a deeper reason a few lines farther down in the poem. "But

51

if there is time," he says, "we shatter the hourglasses." And, of course, there is Time—the Robert Penn Warren-capital-T sort of Time, which is the real problem. This recognition of Time and the horror it works on each of us, sparks the vandalism of the gravestones. There is fear in this act and also anger. "We shatter the hourglasses," he says, "slaughter lambs asleep on children's graves." Elisabeth Kubler-Ross, in her ground-breaking book *On Death and Dying*, tells us that anger is an integral part of the process of grief, anger at the fact of death and anger at the dead person himself. Though we love the dead, we also hate the dead for leaving us and, perhaps, for illustrating so vividly our own future:

> The ancient Hebrews regarded the body of a dead person as something unclean and not to be touched. The early American Indians talked about "evil spirits" and shot arrows into the air to drive the spirits away. Many other cultures have rituals to take care of the "bad" dead person, and they all originate in this feeling of anger which still exists in all of us, though we dislike admitting it. The tradition of the tombstone may originate in this wish to keep the bad spirits deep down in the ground.

I published this poem in a little magazine called *Antaeus*, then again a year or so later in my first book, *Shooting Rats at the Bibb County Dump*. Some short time after that book appeared, I received a letter from an elderly gentleman in Macon. His name was Calder Payne. A few years after I'd left Macon, an effort was made by the Middle Georgia Historical Society to publicize the condition of Rose Hill, to restore it, and to insure that it was properly maintained. Mr. Payne was instrumental in this effort, and his letter detailed, complete with newspaper clippings, much of the damage done to the cemetery and the progress his organization had made toward putting the cemetery right. I thought all of this was wonderful news until I reached the point of his letter. He'd read my book and my poem "Wrestling Angels," and he wanted to know why I'd done it. Why, he demanded, had I vandalized Rose Hill Cemetery? Was I on dope, in some satanic cult, or what?

I'm working from memory here. I no longer have Mr. Payne's letter. However, I remember clearly my shock that anyone would have read my poem so literally. Initially I didn't know quite how to respond. I gave it a day or so, then wrote back to Mr. Payne and praised his fine work at Rose Hill, which was indeed praiseworthy. I detailed some of my intentions in writing my poem and explained that I'd only used first person in order to achieve a greater sense of immediacy, to make the poem more convincing, more real. I loved Rose Hill too, I said, and I certainly had never vandalized that cemetery or any other. Within a very short time, no more than a week, I received his reply. "I don't believe you," he wrote. There was, he said, simply too much detail in the poem for it not to have been based on an actual event.

Apparently Mr. Payne really didn't believe me. Two or three months later I got word from friends in Macon that he was conducting tours of the cemetery—Rose Hill Rambles, he called them—in part to raise money for restorations. It seems he was in the habit of reading my poem to his tour group at the beginning of his "Ramble," then pointing to me as one of the vandals who now made these restorations necessary. I bore no ill will toward Mr. Payne, whose intentions were entirely good.

* * *

Most of us would agree that the existence of God or an afterlife is way beyond the purview of science and can't be verified by empirical investigation. Still, I've always been fascinated with the extravagant attempts Yeats made to contact the other world, his experiments with seances, automatic writing, and spirit machines. In the early eighties this fascination, coupled with a TV documentary narrated by Raymond Burr, sparked a poem of mine called "Recording the Spirit Voices." I don't remember much about that documentary, only that Raymond Burr told the story of certain psychic researchers who had set up recording equipment in a graveyard in hopes of recording the voices of the dead. They caught, I believe, a certain thready murmur that spoke of being in a fearful place. It sounds farfetched sure, but it served pretty well for an hour of cheap programming. It also gave me the notion of taking a portable tape recorder down to Rose Hill Cemetery and hiding it under a tombstone. I can't recall any details of this now, or even where the stone rests. The only clues I have are in the poem itself. The first stanza sets the scene:

> In the hollow below the hill vaults
> I have placed a recorder
> on the grave of a young woman killed in a fire
> and have crouched under the arm of this angel
> to wait for voices,
> tree frogs whirring through the blue pines,
> the Ocmulgee lapping the bank at the foot of Rose Hill.

What I find interesting about this poem now is the more or less straightforward statement it makes about the poet as seeker. The world is always trying to tell the poet something, Warren suggests, but here the persona isn't just listening. He's actively seeking, trying to catch by stealth the secrets the world would keep. The second stanza says it:

A gray moon over the Confederate graves
gleams on the water,
the white gallon jugs floating some man's trotline.
Like me he's trying to bring things to the surface
where they don't belong.

This is the sort of thing that can have its consequences. At a Dublin séance in 1888, Yeats is reported to have been seized by a spirit or, at least, by the spirit of the moment, and to have had his head banged violently on the table repeatedly. This, understandably, put him off séances for several years. Nothing like that happens here, thank goodness, but the persona does feel an odd sense of anxiety. We're accustomed to thinking of the afterlife as a pleasant place, free of trouble, pain, and fear, and the landscaping and architecture of our cemeteries, the epitaphs we cut into our gravestones, usually reinforce our notions of a peaceful rest. However, other possibilities have troubled us. Prince Hamlet speaks of "the dread of something after death, the undiscover'd country, from whose bourn/No traveller returns." And who, having read either Homer or Dante, could much blame him. The twentieth century psychoanalyst Carl Jung, in his wonderful memoir *Memories, Dreams, Reflections,* calls the afterlife "grand and terrible," and we continue to express our anxieties about it through gothic novels and horror movies. Witness the classic *Night of the Living Dead.*

As the poem ends the persona feels something of this anxiety, a dread, even a fear that he might actually discover some evidence of a life after death:

> Across the river
> blue needles rasp like the voices
> I heard on television,
> the documented whisper of spirits, *I'm afraid here, I'm afraid.*
> So am I now
> as leaves in the hollow rustle their dry tongues
> afraid to hear a woman scream from a burning house
> to record some evidence her tombstone lied,
> bury the truth these angels stand on: born and died.

* * *

A year or so after I discovered Rose Hill, the rise of the Allman Brothers Band added another dimension to my experience of the place. Duane and Greg Allman, Dickey Betts, Berry Oakley, Butch Trucks, and Jaimoe Johnson were a group of musicians who had jammed around Florida without great commercial success until Phil Walden brought them all to Macon and Capricorn Records. What came out of that union made rock music history and rivaled, perhaps, even the success Walden had enjoyed with Otis Redding. I attended, I believe, the first concert the band gave as The Allman Brothers Band. That would have been in the fall of 1969, in Willingham Chapel at Mercer, and I had a front row seat because my friend Allen Osborne worked for Walden, who was a fraternity brother of ours, and told me to get there early. I had tried to break into several little bands myself and even entertained the idea of becoming a professional rock musician. As odd as that sounds now, during the sixties that was the dream of most everyone who could play three clean chords on a guitar. Fortunately, the first few notes Duane Allman hit that night on his gold Les Paul disabused me entirely of that dream. I had never heard anything like the Allman Brothers Band, and neither had many other people.

The Allmans quickly took to Rose Hill Cemetery, which they found fertile ground, and several songs came out of their experiences there, notably "In Memory of Elizabeth Reed," a Dickey Betts tune, and "Little Martha," the only song Duane Allman ever wrote. Duane took the title from a statue of a little girl standing over the grave of Martha Ellis, who had died in 1896, at the age of twelve. Sometime in the mid-nineties I visited Macon again with the critic Ernest Suarez, who was writing an article on Allman. We'd been listening to Allman's song, and I took Suarez down to Rose Hill to see Martha Ellis' grave. We'd talked with several old friends of the band, notably Kirk West, long time road manager, and learned that fans often left candy, coins, and toys on her grave, interesting remnants, I thought, of very old notions of the afterlife. That thought and my own anxieties about middle age and what lay beyond it kindled a little poem I called "At the Grave of Martha Ellis." The first stanza puts the reader in place and time. Place: Rose Hill. Time: spring. The second stanza addresses the statue of the girl and touches on the question of rebirth, the most obvious and insistent message of spring:

> Little Martha,
> in middle age rebirth isn't such easy work,
> though everything goes at it again
> like Baptists reeling to articulate rapture,
> and the morning reissues its pledge—
> the mockingbird,
> the crow breaking the far hush of the wind,
> and in the valley above the river,
> white clouds of dogwood floating through the underbrush
> while redwings drop like blood
> through the branches.

"In middle age," truly, "rebirth isn't such easy work," and yet everything in the natural world goes go about it yearly in a frenzied way. The world, much to our amazement, desperately insists on this uncanny process of regeneration, which makes Rose Hill Cemetery a beautiful place in the spring. The irony here never ceases to tease and amaze me. A few lines from a newer poem called "Easter Shoes Epistle" focus the question:

> Every spring
> the world is such a tricky magician, tugging whole maple trees
> out of its black silk hat, pulling thunderstorms
> from its sleeve . . .
> Miracle or sleight of hand
> is what I fret about.

"Miracle or sleight of hand," yes, and the question we ask ourselves is the obvious question of parallels. What coy or secretive intellect guides that process of regeneration? And how does this inform the ultimate message of the graveyard?

* * *

Rose Hill Cemetery was, in short, my first haunted landscape. In this role it has been faithful for more than thirty years. Most recently it turned up in a poem I wrote about the Allman Brothers. A few years ago I had the opportunity to spend the night in the old "Big House" on Vineville Avenue, which was one of the first homes of the band. It's owned now by my friends Kirk and Kirsten West, who through their long association with the band have put together a fascinating archive. This overnight stay jarred loose several memories of my early days in Macon, and one of those memories recounts what now seems to me a typical visit to Rose Hill, how I would walk through the cemetery, high on adventure or whatever was available, seeking a voice or a vision, watching for spirits, waiting for ghosts. A few lines catch the scene:

> But perhaps you, too, in some freaked-out greed for vision
> or grace, have found yourself
> > chewing a mouthful of crabgrass, stupefied
> and afraid, skulking on all fours those briary terraces
> of Rose Hill Cemetery to pause on the edge
> of a crumbling wall
> > and see in blue half-moonlight
> the granite slab of Elizabeth Reed tarnishing under the charcoal trees. . .

* * *

I'd stumbled down
those terraces to the bricked crypts bordering the railroad tracks
and river. *Little plazas cool as courtyards,*

Borges says,
                prowling through the mausoleums of Recoleta.
Rhetoric of shadow and marble, inviting enough, sure,
but at night in Rose Hill, in those alleys
of maimed angels, a shabby Victorian dignity bordered on indignation.

Still that music of river and something else . . .
that late bird, far off,
                        like a whistler lonely in the afterworld,
little prelude, little curtain-opener,
and I waited for an hour on a marble tomb,
                                drooling weeds, watching
through a canopy of water oak
the half-moon ringing a light show over the far ridge of pines,
opening act for a no-show.
Looking for the dead? an angel drones,
Don't look here,
                nobody home.

Nobody home, alas, and yet we keep looking because
that's the impulse of the seeker. To the rational mind the
message of Rose Hill may be death, but to that other part,
the part that houses the seeker, that message falls short. For
the seeker something else insinuates itself onto those hills
and terraces. It whispers in the rustle of brush and leaves, in
the sound of the river at the foot of the hill, and if we listen
closely enough, those whispers seem to be coming from the
graves themselves.

THE POETRY OF BRIDGES: GROWING UP SMALL-TOWN, GAZING TOWARD ATLANTA

Robert Penn Warren, born and raised in Guthrie, Kentucky, was asked once if he considered himself to be a Southern writer. His response was, "What else could I be?" By that he meant that the place of his birth and his upbringing had molded his character in a distinct and inconvertible way. His every interaction with the world was colored by the history and social code of his region. This is not to say that he was always proud of that history or that he always agreed with that code, only that he could not live independently of them.

The South is plagued by a great number of misconceptions held by folks in other parts of the world, and all writers born below the Mason-Dixon Line must eventually come to terms with both the myth and the actuality of "The South." This involves facing some disturbing truths concerning intolerance, violence, and racial exploitation. Still, it bears remembering that these human defects are not exclusive to our region. The popular line is that the South has terrible sins in its past and its present, but that it also contains many distinguishing virtues. This is certainly true, but might be said of any part of the world. What distinguishes the American South is the fact that it lost a war fought largely over its intractable immoralities. This seems to me a particularly cogent point when regarding the work of its writers. The South is a wounded region, and the wounded heart always seeks transcendence. When the wound is cultural, the personal response tends to find recourse through religion or art. In this broad sense the post-Civil War South has become a land of preachers and poets.

Any writer who does any amount of public speaking will inevitably be asked how he or she became a writer. And any writer from the South will eventually be asked how growing up there has influenced his or her work. I've pondered these questions because they've always been mysteries to me. I was raised in the 1950s, in the foothills of the north Georgia mountains, and nothing in my family or my community would have ever suggested that I might scribble a word onto a page.

I didn't come from a reading family. In fact, I don't think I ever saw either of my parents reading a book. They were children of the Great Depression, and they worked hard all their lives. The only entertainment they had time for was television, so the only books we had in our house, other than a Bible or two, were my school books. My Granny Ashe was the reader in our family. She had a small library of ten or so novels, and as I like to point out, two of those were Margaret Mitchell's *Gone with the Wind.* She had a hardback and a well-worn paperback.

Nevertheless, I did grow up loving to read. This was because of my mother's encouragement and a little bookstore that belonged to my second grade teacher. As a boy, though, I spent most of my spare time playing sports—in my case baseball. Playing sports was expected of a boy in a small town such as Canton, while books, serious music, art, and almost anything called cultural were deeply suspect. If not reined in, they were pursuits that might eventually take issue with the doctrines of fundamentalist Christianity.

We lived in the Bible Belt, and sometimes it felt like we lived right on the hardest part of the buckle. An irony here is the fact that my earliest memories concerning poetic language go back to church, to the mid-1950s and the Canton First Baptist Church. I'm talking, of course, about the wonderful imagery in those old Baptist hymns and the beautiful and antique language of the King James Bible. This is where I first saw language work figuratively, where I first experienced language as art. In many ways it was the sort of introduction I could have received only in a small town such as Canton.

2

Atlanta, about forty miles south on Georgia 5, was a radically different place. It was a place of culture. It had museums, libraries, colleges, art galleries, a symphony. The state house was there, and under its gold dome legislators made the laws that ruled the state. But more than all of this Atlanta had a history, a history that had evolved into a powerful myth.

During my early childhood, the first historical event to really impress me was the American Civil War. In elementary school the notebooks of my classmates were covered with doodles of the Confederate battle flag, and at home my grandmother told stories about women she'd known in her childhood who'd actually witnessed General William Tecumseh Sherman's troops burning their way through Georgia. My experience was far from unique, and my friends and I drew a certain common identity from all of this, without knowing very much about the actual causes and execution of that war. Things simply were what they were, and we found ourselves, inexplicably, part of a culture where Blacks lived and worked on one side of a deep chasm and Whites on the other. It all had to do with history, and our primary connection to that history was the city of Atlanta, a mysterious place few of us had ever visited.

My first memory of that city was a trip to the Fox Theater. I was twelve years old when my best friend's mother drove us to a matinee showing of the movie *Gone with the Wind*. The Fox was easily the most exotic building I'd ever seen. Built in the 1920s as the headquarters for the Yaarab Shriners of Atlanta, its mixture of Islamic and Egyptian architecture made it a very strange presence on Peachtree Street.

The movie we saw that Sunday was exotic in a completely different way. "Gone with the Wind," of course, popularized the myth of the "Lost Cause" and the Confederates who fought to preserve the values of the Old South. I bought into it, as did most of my friends, or a large part of it anyway, though we all felt a nagging sense that something was wrong with that picture, just as something was wrong with the society we lived in. At least one group of Southerners, those folks on the other side of the chasm, viewed history from an entirely different perspective, and they had found a powerful voice rising from a pulpit in Atlanta, a voice that was starting to build a cultural bridge. That pulpit belonged to the Ebenezer Baptist Church on Auburn Avenue, and the voice belonged to The Rev. Dr. Martin Luther King, Jr.

Oddly enough my own experiments with language and poetry began around the time I first became aware of the Civil Rights Movement. Some of this, of course, is simply coincidence. I was a teenager and just becoming aware of my world and feeling the need to express my feelings on paper. But as I remember, a very large number of those early attempts at poetry dealt with social injustice, racial and otherwise.

My generation is the last to have lived in a segregated South, and on the streets of Canton in the 1950s and early 60s I rarely saw a black person. In fact, no one I knew talked much about race. What I learned of the Movement as a teenager came mostly in snippets from the TV news.

A few names became familiar—Martin Luther King, Joseph Lowery, Andrew Young—but the knowledge I was able to gather about the African-American struggle wasn't deep. These snippets, however, served not only to reinforce the questions I had about the *status quo* in the South, they also created an empathy that led me to books such as James Baldwin's *Blues for Mr. Charlie* and Ralph Ellison's *Invisible Man.*

For most of my teenage years the struggle for civil rights was something that happened in Atlanta and other large cities. The people I knew had no idea what was happening in the local black churches or the Ralph Bunche School, and they were shocked when the African-American community attempted to desegregate the Canton Theater. There was some violence—a car was turned over in the street—and the threat of much more, but no one was seriously hurt. That was just about the extent of my personal experience with the struggle for civil rights. Atlanta was my connection, my bridge to a greater awareness of the human community and the growing role I would need to play in it.

And speaking of bridges. My wife and I recently saw a news story on television about a young boy asking President Obama why so many people hated him. The President hugged the boy and told him this was mostly politics and people didn't really hate him. This was a crystallizing moment, a painful reminder that some people still lag behind, but also a hopeful reminder that enduring bridges have been built. President Obama was not elected solely by African-Americans, but by all Americans.

A few years ago young writer asked me why I hadn't written more about race. I scratched my head and told her that all poems were about race because, on some level, all poems are about humanity. Basically, the message I've taken from poetry is this. There is only the one life—the one life with infinite variations. We all share that life—we're born, we aspire, we struggle, we search for meaning, we die. Poetry is the art of metaphor, which is the art of making connections, the art of discovering bridges. Poetry's great message is the message of commonality, of our fundamental humanity, the significance of being a human creature at our particular moment.

SHOOTING RATS, DROPPING BUNTS, AND BREAKING IN: THREE EARLY POEMS

S hooting Rats at the Bibb County Dump" is a very early poem, which first appeared in *Harper's* in the mid-seventies. It's was an odd poem then, I think, in its choice of subject, and it set the tone for much of my early work. A few years later it became the title poem of my first book. Fairly quickly, as the reviews came out, I was tagged "the Laureate of the Rednecks," which some reviewers said with humor and affection for the poems, but others said with neither humor nor affection. The *Atlanta Journal-Constitution* review cast me into the pit of male chauvinism with James Dickey, Harry Crews, and other folks the reviewer considered unsavory Southern sorts, an unfair and painful charge against all named. It was a mean-spirited review all around and came complete with an illustration of a young man holding a whiskey bottle while leaning against the fin of a '57 Chevy—just in case the readers of the AJC didn't know what a redneck looked like. Mostly, though, the reviews were quite favorable, and I was deeply pleased that a number of my favorite poets liked the book, Robert Penn Warren and James Dickey among them. Shortly after it came out, Dickey told me that in the title poem I'd created just about as much sympathy anyone could create—for a rat.

The poem came out of an experience I had as a freshmen in college. I went to school at Mercer University, a small, private liberal arts college in Macon, Georgia. At that time Mercer had a student body of maybe 1500, mostly kids from Georgia, but a good number also from Florida and other parts of the South. Mercer was, and remains, a Southern Baptist school, but in the late 1960s, when I entered, it was liberal beyond any dream of my mother or father, who sent me there in hopes that I wouldn't be corrupted by the dangerous social trends infecting the country. The son of our Baptist minister, a high school classmate of mine, was going there, so they pictured Mercer as a safe enough place. Fraternities were still a large part of social life then, and during my first year at Mercer I pledged Phi Delta Theta. These fellows weren't exactly the scholars on campus, nor were they the Gant shirt crowd. They were party guys, a group of fellows not very unlike the fraternity depicted in the John Belushi movie *Animal House*. My first semester I made two Cs and a D, the D in English composition, and for the next two years I did little more than drink beer, listen to the Allman Brothers, and involve myself in various fraternity shenanigans. One of the more bizarre involved the Bibb County dump. On Friday and Saturday nights when the guys had taken their dates back to Wesleyan College or the women's dorm—those, of course, who could get dates—they'd load whatever beer or whiskey they had left into two or three cars and drive out to the county dump to shoot rats. Over the years, as I came to discover, this had developed into something of a ritual in the fraternity, perhaps even what one might call a folk art.

What little I remember of that place is a long wasted field of red clay strewn with various sorts of junk, a field maybe twice the size of a football field, maybe larger. At the far end of that field sat two or three huge mounds of garbage, twenty-five or thirty feet high, depending on the time of the month and whether or not the bulldozers had started to plow it under. Not sacks of garbage, as I remember, but loose garbage of all sorts—rotting food, old clothes, whatever—pushed up into small mountains. The smell wasn't pleasant, and in Macon, Georgia, the wind hardly blows.

I don't remember much else about the landscape, except that as these guys reached the edge of the field, they'd cut off their headlights. After a few seconds maybe, the stars or the moon might highlight the field and the various junk scattered here and there. Then the little caravan of cars or trucks would roll in slowly, no more than a crawl, dodging as best as they could the old truck tires, broken furniture, whatever else lay in their path. When they got within firing distance, which depended largely on how drunk they were, they'd pull their cars into a line paralleling the mounds and cut their engines. Someone, though, would always leave on an accessory switch.

Most had .22 rifles, a few had pistols, but shotguns were strictly prohibited. Not sporting, of course, and in the South sportsmanship is everything. They'd squat then in front of their bumpers and wait. Several minutes might pass in absolute silence. Maybe you'd hear only the wind in the pines around the edges of the dump, or someone belching in the near dark. Then very quietly a sort of scratching sound would come to the opposite ends of the garbage. Slowly it would gather strength and move toward the center, getting louder and louder, and after another minute or so the huge mounds of garbage would simply be swarming with it. Someone would rise quietly then, lean into a car, and jerk on the headlights. And there they were—dozens and dozens of little red eyes frozen in the light. Then blam! blam! blam!— which lasted only a very short time, a minute or two, because even a rat will eventually figure out that something is amiss and crawl off into the dark.

Years later I remembered that and thought, perhaps for the first time, how strange and disturbing that was. In the poem I wanted to turn things around on the fellows with the guns. I wanted to show how they really didn't have anything on those rats, how they too were heading, unawares, out toward the same dark fate. This poem, I think, was one of my first flirtations with irony, the common sort of insight, I suppose, that young people take to be profound. This is the way it came out:

Shooting Rats at the Bibb County Dump

Loaded on beer and whiskey, we ride
to the dump in carloads
to turn our headlights across the wasted field,
freeze the startled eyes of rats against mounds of rubbish.

Shot in the head, they jump only once, lie still like dead beer cans.
Shot in the gut or rump, they writhe and try to burrow
into garbage, hide in old truck tires,
rusty oil drums, cardboard boxes scattered across the mounds,
or else dag themselves on forelegs across our beams of light
toward the darkness at the edge of the dump.

It's the light they believe kills.
We drink and load again, let them crawl
for all they're worth into the darkness we're headed for.

2

When I was a boy I played a great deal of baseball, not because I was an exceptional second baseman or shortstop—I wasn't—but because my father was a fanatic about baseball. In high school he was actually a star football player, a very fast and crafty halfback, and football may have been his first love, but I was always too small to play that game, and baseball was a game where agility could be a substitute for size. So we played baseball, and from the time I was seven years old until I was eighteen and leaving home to go to college, I played in at least one organized league a year and sometimes two.

We lived in a small shingled house on the side of Highway 5, in Canton, Georgia, about a hundred yards south of my grandfather's country store. Just across the road from us there was a used car lot and beyond that an open field that belonged to my grandfather. Around the time I started playing ball, my father turned that field into a regulation Little League Baseball diamond. He built a twelve-foot wire backstop and boarded in half of the outfield. A tall bank bordering a neighbor's garden provided the rest of the fence. With the exception of a small drainage ditch that ran across the outfield, it was a nice field, and a good many of the Little League teams practiced there during the summers.

My dad and I practiced there almost every dry day. When 6 o'clock came around and he was due home from work, I knew where I needed to be. That was beside the front door, with the practice bag and gloves. We'd walk across the road and the graveled lot of Carmichael Motors, and he'd hit me grounders and throw batting practice for an hour or so, sometimes longer. And very often he'd stress the techniques and strategies of bunting. My father loved the idea of the bunt. I could've hit a double every time I came up to the plate, and he'd still have preached the necessity of the bunt, the necessity of sacrificing for the good of the team.

Many years later I remembered all of this, and I had one of my rare epiphanies. I remember thinking, *Wow, this man spent a lot of time with me*. He must have been exhausted at the end of the day, and he had very serious war wounds that still troubled him. Still, day in and day out, we persisted at this for years. Finally, I came to understand that this whole routine had, perhaps, very little to do with baseball. He was not an articulate man, his emotions rarely found words, and baseball was simply his way of communicating. I started playing with some baseball language then, and the poem that came out of that is called "Sign for My Father, Who Stressed the Bunt." The seed of the poem was the play on the word "sacrifice," and as was fairly typical for me at the time, the first line that came became the last line of the poem.

Sign for My Father, Who Stressed the Bunt

On the rough diamond, the hand-cut field
below dog lot and barn, we rehearsed the strict technique of bunting.
I watched from the infield,

the mound, the backstop
as your left hand climbed the bat, your legs
and shoulders squared toward the pitcher.
You could drop it like a seed
down either baseline.
I admired your style, but not enough
to take my eyes off the bank that served as our centerfield fence.

Years passed, three leagues of organized ball, no few lives.
I could homer into the garden
beyond the bank, into the left-field lot of Carmichael Motors,
and still you stressed the same technique, the crouch
and spring, the lead arm absorbing just enough impact.
That whole tiresome pitch
about basics never changing,
and I never learned what you were laying down.

Like a hand brushed across the bill of a cap,
let this be the sign
I'm getting a grip on the sacrifice.

3

Three quick things about my father. First of all, I'm not the real David Bottoms. My father is. I'm only the junior version. Second, when he was in high school, my dad was not what anyone would call a great scholar. However, as I've said, he was an outstanding athlete. He was a track star and held a number of state records, but he excelled especially in football. He was a star running back, and won in his last year in school a football scholarship to Mercer University, which had a pretty good team at that time. In fact, he was such a great runner, they held him back for two years at Canton High School to play ball. And I often think had it not been for World War II, he might still be there hobbling out of the backfield. But the war did come along and that brings up point number three. With his best friend, he joined the navy. He shipped out of San Francisco on the USS *Atlanta*, which was the prototype of a new heavily-armed light cruiser, and for about five months the *Atlanta* had a distinguished service record in the Pacific theater—the Solomon Islands, the Guadalcanal-Tugali landings, the capture and defense of Guadalcanal—until the night of November 13, 1942. That would have been Friday the 13th, November 1942.

The *Atlanta* was part of an American task force that sailed north through a little strip of water between Florida Island and Guadalcanal when, in the middle of the night, it ran head on into what the U.S. Naval Department calls a "superior Japanese surface presence." This means essentially that the Japanese had more boats than we did. A Japanese destroyer flashed a spotlight onto the deck of the *Atlanta*, and the *Atlanta* spun its guns and shot it out. That began the naval battle of Guadalcanal, which is often called the fiercest naval battle in the history of warfare. The *Atlanta* quickly took 49 shells and two torpedoes. Much of the superstructure of the ship was blown away and over a third of the crew was wounded or killed. My dad was stationed in the upper gun turret on the ship's stern, turret number six. That turret took five direct hits, but I suspect it was the first one that blew him out the door and onto the deck. I read in the local paper a few years ago that the last thing he remembered was someone strapping a life jacket onto him and throwing him into the ocean. He'd taken severe head wounds, side wounds, and leg wounds, and he floated around for an unknown length of time, unconscious, until his best friend jumped out of a lifeboat and swam out, against all odds that he was alive, and pulled him in. The next two months of his life were spent in a hospital bed in Guam, the next nine months in a hospital bed in San Francisco. That was the end of his athletic career and his education at Mercer, the school he eventually sent me to.

But this poem is not really about all of that. I've gone somewhat around the side of the barn. It's not really about my father, but about me—about my first day in the sixth grade at Canton Elementary School. That would have been Miss Sarah Rhymer's room. I remember being the first person to show up for the class, standing in that door, and looking out over that empty classroom, looking for the desk that just mine. Well, being who I was then, I looked, of course, to the back of the room, to the last row—and not only there, but to the desk beside the window. And when I walked back there and sat down, I experienced something out of the "Twilight Zone." Sure enough, it was my desk, because when I looked down, I saw that my name was carved about half an inch deep into the desktop. I pondered that all day, and eventually figured out that the building in which I attended elementary school was the building in which my father attended high school. He, of course, had gone before me.

"The Desk" is a poem about remembering that desktop some twenty-five years later in an alcoholically induced state of nostalgia, and about deciding that it was, indeed, meant to be mine, that I had, perhaps, a certain moral authority that exceeded the legal authority exercised by the Cherokee County Board of Education. The poem is about going back to that school building late one night, say between the hours of twelve and one, with a flashlight, a hammer, and a

crowbar, to reclaim for my own that which some higher
authority no doubt meant for me to have.

The Desk

Under the fire escape, crouched, one knee in cinders,
I pulled the ball-peen hammer from my belt,
cracked a square of window pane,
the gummed latch, and swung the window,
crawled through that stone hole into the boiler room
of Canton Elementary School, once Canton High,
where my father served three extra years
as star halfback and sprinter.
Behind a flashlight's
cane of light, I climbed a staircase almost a ladder
and found a door. On the second nudge of my shoulder,
it broke into a hallway dark as history,
as whose end lay the classroom I had studied
over and over in the deep obsession of memory.

I swept that room with my light—an empty blackboard,
a metal table, a half-globe lying on the floor
like a punctured basketball—then followed
that beam across the rows of desks,
the various catalogs of lovers, the lists
of all those who would and would not do what,
until it stopped on the corner desk of the back row,
and I saw again, after many years the name
of my father, my name, carved deep into the oak top.

To gauge the depth I ran my finger across that scar,
and wondered at the dreams he must have lived
as his eyes ran back and forth
from the cinder yard below the window
to the empty practice field
to the blade of his pocket knife etching carefully

the long, angular lines of his name,
the dreams he must have laid out one behind another
like yard lines, in the dull, pre-practice afternoons
of geography and civics, before he ever dreamed
of Savo Sound or Guadalcanal.
                                    In honor of dreams
I sank to my knees on the smooth, oiled floor,
and stood my flashlight on its end.
Half the yellow circle lit the underedge of the desk,
the other threw a half-moon on the ceiling,
and in that split light I tapped the hammer
easy up the overhang of the desk top. Nothing gave
but the walls' sharp echo, so I swung again,
and again harder, and harder still in half anger
rising to anger at the stubborn joint, losing all fear
of my first crime against the city, the county,
the state, whatever government claimed dominion,
until I had hammered up in the ringing dark
a salvo of crossfire, and on a frantic recoil glanced
the flashlight, the classroom spinning black
as a coma.
            I've often pictured the face of the teacher
whose student first pointed to that topless desk,
the shock of a slow hand rising from the back row,
their eyes meeting over the question of absence.
I've wondered too if some low authority of the system
discovered that shattered window,
and finding no typewriters, no business machines,
no audiovisual gear missing, failed to account for it,
so let it pass as minor vandalism.
I've heard nothing.
And rarely do I fret when I see that oak scar leaning
against my basement wall, though I wonder what it means
to own my father's name.

INTERVIEWS

THE POETRY RECEIVER:
An Interview Conducted by
Deborah Browning and Capers Limehouse

This interview, commissioned for the initial issue of *The Atlanta Review*, took place in March 1994 on the campus of Georgia State University in Atlanta.

Browning: Could we start by asking about your progenitors? I wonder if you can trace specific instances of their influence in your poetry, or is the influence more unconscious?

Bottoms: The first real influence I remember, and it was a large one, was when I was a student at Mercer University. Everybody at Mercer in the late '60s was writing like Dylan Thomas. And so was I. I was writing very bad, good-sounding poems. My initial impulse was musical, all my poems were coming from sounds. I thought if you came up with a great line and you put thirteen more behind it, you had a sonnet, and a sonnet was a poem. So I wrote a lot of poems like that. Then I'd go back two weeks later and read them again and find them totally incomprehensible. About my senior year, when I was editing the school literary magazine, I found a new direction. I met my very first living poet, a man named James Seay, who teaches now at Chapel Hill. Jim had just published his first book, *Let Not Your Hart*, and he had come to Mercer to do a reading. It was the first poetry reading I'd ever heard, and I was pretty amazed. Jim is a very striking figure—a tall, thin guy with long, blond hair and a black eye-patch over his eye. Very swashbuckling. Just what you might picture a poet to look like. He was born in Panola County, Mississippi, and his poems had a strong narrative content. I really liked them, and I latched onto him. I was trying to learn something. We spent three or four days together while he was in Macon, and I think he directed me to the poems of James Dickey. Then I started reading Warren and other Southerners. But from that point on I made a conscious effort in my poems to change the direction they were going. I stopped looking for poems in sound, and I started looking for them in the situations of my life. And suddenly they started to have some content. They started to mean something.

Browning: I'd call that an identifiable influence.

Bottoms: James Dickey was a big influence also. But that was later on. I think when I was in my early 20s, I was too stupid to know how good Dickey's poems really are. I've heard a number of Southern poets say—poets mostly of the generation before me—that Dickey's work was just so good that they felt discouraged reading it. A professor I had at Florida State told me that once early in his career he was trying to do the same sort of thing Dickey was doing and after reading Dickey he felt like he had to change his whole approach. Dickey intimidated a lot of writers in this way. I'm lucky, I think, because there are 25 or 26 years between us, and I was too dumb to be intimidated. I just went on and did what I felt like doing.

Limehouse: I wonder if you were just being self-protective?

Bottoms: Maybe. But I didn't discover the real force of his poems until I was in my late twenties, I guess.

Browning: So you didn't let his influence thwart your early development.

Bottoms: That's right. I know I learned a great deal from him, but I don't think I knew enough then to let his poems frighten me off my home turf. Does that make sense?

Limehouse: Yes. So do you think now that you write like Dickey in any way?

Bottoms: Actually, I don't. We've written about the same things occasionally—we're from the same part of the country, and we have many of the same interests, and because of that people like to toss us into the same boat—but we don't approach things in the same way. Fred Chappell said one time that he thought Dickey and I were about as far apart as you could get in terms of our approach. I think he's right. He said that Dickey writes these big, expansive poems, and I write these muscular, compressed poems. Dickey tends to expand and I tend to compress. My approach is actually a lot closer to James Wright or to Theodore Roethke. But I love Dickey's poems and he's been a great and positive influence.

Browning: There's been a lot of talk recently about the role of narrative in poetry. I heard you say something once about the "narrative surface" of a poem. What did you mean by that?

Bottoms: Well, I meant just that. All of my poems depend heavily on narrative, but I mean it to work only as a surface for the poem. A lot of stuff goes into poetry—I know that. But what has always been most fascinating for me is the way language can work figuratively. Narrative is interesting but it's not enough. You can open up any literary magazine these days and find a poem that's just a little story chopped up into 25 or 30 lines. To me that's not what poetry is all about. I want the poem to discover something beyond the literal, and the narrative provides an opportunity for that. It provides a context in which the language can work metaphorically. What I mean is this—a good poet can find ways of embedding triggers in the narrative surface to make the language leap into another level of meaning.

Limehouse: Could you talk about that in terms of "Under the Vulture-tree," say, or "Sign for My Father," poems that seem to be successful in that way?

Bottoms: Well, that baseball poem depends entirely on word-play. The figurative meaning develops out of a series of puns that come near the end of the poem. By the time the reader hits the last word "sacrifice," he or she has come to understand that the poem is not so much about learning to bunt as it is about the sacrifice the father has made for the son. The narrative surface—the story about the father teaching the boy to bunt—is interesting, of course, but to me it's really important only in the way it works figuratively in the poem. That's what we can in my classes the DHM, the Deep Hidden Meaning, a phrase I lifted from my friend Jim Seay. And it's the word play that allows the figurative possibility to reveal itself.

Limehouse: So the narrative just provides a literal level for the poem?

Bottoms: Yes, usually. The poem has to work literally first. Another interesting thing about narrative, though, is that it can operate figuratively itself, apart from language. This occurs when the narrative pattern of the poem touches the mythic or the archetypal.

Browning: Can you give us an example of that—one of your poems?

Bottoms: I'd point to that poem "Under the Boathouse." When the swimmer in the poem dives to the bottom of the lake and gets caught on a fish hook, he follows the pattern of submersion, symbolic death, and resurrection. The pattern itself is archetypal—like baptism. I think Carl Jung called it the "myth of the night journey," or something like that. A good example is the Old Testament story of Jonah—the big fish swallows Jonah, takes him down to a symbolic death, then surfaces and spits him out into a new life. The pattern repeats itself in any number of myths.

Browning: I heard you say once that people accuse you of having "hard closures." What exactly do they mean by that? Do they mean the poem ends too neatly?

Bottoms: Yes, I think so. Maybe "accuse" isn't exactly the right word, but people have said that. Often my poems will turn near the end and try to make a figurative leap there. But not always. I do like that, though, because it seems to give the poem a final punch, a final burst of energy. I remember someone writing in *Poetry*—somebody reviewing *Under the Vulture-Tree*—that these poems didn't strain for closure the way some of the earlier ones had, and he liked that. But I don't remember making any conscious effort at that. I haven't experimented much with form or approach in my poems. I hit on what I wanted to do relatively early, I think, and I've been pretty content in my efforts to try to perfect it. And that's okay.

Limehouse: We did want to ask a question about how you've changed over the years. Do you feel like you compete with our earlier self in any way or that people expect you to?

Bottoms: Yes, I think so. If you write some stuff you like and live long enough to look back at it from a distance, you'll always feel like you're competing with yourself. I'd like to write another poem as good as "Vulture-Tree" or "Under the Boathouse." But maybe I have and I just don't know it. After taking time out for two novels [*Any Cold Jordan* and *Easter Weekend*], I'm writing poems again, and I like some of them very much.

Limehouse: Is that a difficult transition?

Bottoms: For me it is. It requires a totally different kind of imagination. For me it's very hard to write fiction, to concern myself with everything that goes into a novel, the fleshing out of a situation, characterization, plot, then go work on a poem, which is a distilling, a condensing.

Browning: So you think that the two processes are more dissonant, that they don't really inform each other?

Bottoms: To me they seem almost opposites. I much prefer writing poems to writing fiction. Maybe I'm just better at it, I don't know, but I much prefer the poems.

Limehouse: You said it takes a different sort of imagination. What do you mean by that?

Bottoms: Maybe sensibility is a better word. Fiction and poetry are just made in different ways. Fiction is arduous work. It requires a long commitment to the page. Okay, say you plot your novel out in a few weeks, but then you work on it every day, from nine to five, for two or three years. You don't work eight hours a day for a year on poems. You work just as hard, I think, but it's a different kind of labor. The imaginative experience is much more intense. People who say they sit down at their typewriters every morning at nine to write poems are suspicious to me. Most poems just don't come that way.

Limehouse: Where do they come from?

Bottoms: Well, I'm not sure I know. I wish I could just go to the kitchen faucet and turn it on and have a poem come out, but that's not what happens. They come from the world, of course, but they also come through the poet.

Browning: Are you saying that the poet receives the poem in some way?

Bottoms: Yes, I see the poet as sort of a poetry-receiver, the same way your stereo has an FM receiver. But you don't get the poem all at once the way your stereo picks up something off WABE. What you get from the world is an initial signal that a poem needs to be written. You take that signal, that idea or image or phrase, and you take it to your typewriter or your word processor or your No. 2 pencil and you flesh it out. You apply what you know about writing and try to make a poem out of it. The trick, I think is learning to recognize the signal. The trick is tuning in.

Browning: And how do you do that?

Bottoms: I think it has to do with the way you lead your life. First of all, you read and you learn how poems work. Then you simply make yourself as receptive to the world as you can. You watch for the signals to come in, and you wait. Randall Jarrell described it as standing out in a thunderstorm and waiting to be hit by lightning. Seamus Heaney talks about the same thing in a very fine essay called "Feeling into Words." He calls it "divining" and compares the poet to a water diviner. But you don't sit down at the typewriter cold and expect to write a poem. You'll be there all day staring at a blank page, or just simply at a collection of words that don't mean very much.

Limehouse: I'm interested in the time issue, maybe because we are basically the same age. I wonder about this thing of being middle-aged. It seems to me that we live in a culture where it's difficult to be a middle-aged poet. I don't know what we're supposed to be when we're over 40. Do you ever get that sense?

Bottoms: I don't know. I edited a book with Dave Smith called *The Morrow Anthology of Younger American Poets* [1985], so I'm at least partly guilty of promoting some of that younger writer stuff. And now I'm not a young poet anymore. The Yale folks sort of defined the term for us, didn't they? After forty you can't win the Yale award. In some ways I don't mind all the emphasis on younger poets—the Lavan Younger poet, the Yale Younger poet, *The Morrow Anthology*—because writers who are starting out need encouragement. But what we middle-aged folks have to remember is simply this—it's not a race. Good poems are written by poets of all ages. And the poem is all that counts.

Limehouse: But don't you think there's also this sense in our society, especially for artists, that you have some sort of special creative genius when you're in your early twenties, like Keats, and if you miss that moment, it's just too late?

Bottoms: Maybe there's some of that. But I don't think of poets in that way. Look at the late poems of Warren. Nothing he wrote in his twenties can stand up to *Audubon* or *Now and Then*. I think I know what you mean though. There's a strange phase a writer passes into when he or she can't barter on promise any longer. Suddenly you're not a promising young writer anymore, but you're not distinguished yet either, you haven't yet developed your complete potential. There you are, just a writer, hopefully a good one, but nevertheless a writer who's stuck between promise and real accomplishment. And it's a frightening phase to find yourself in because there's a much larger leap between good and distinguished than there is between promising and good.

Browning: Haven't we touched on the question of ambition here?

Bottoms: Yes, but it's a foolish question. Any ambition beyond the poem itself is misdirection. And dangerous.

Browning: Dangerous in what way?

Bottoms: In the sense that ambition beyond the page interferes. Too many people in this country see poetry as a career. That sounds strange to say, but colleges are full of them. Poetry is an art. You shouldn't go into an MFA program to get a degree and land a job. You should go to hone your writing skills. There are careerists and politicians in all the arts, and poetry's no different. But none of that stuff makes your poems any better. Or your paintings, or your music.

Limehouse: What do you think it means to be Southern in terms of your being a poet? People do tend to label poets as "Southern." Do you think it matters? Also, can you contrast how living in the South might be at work in your poetry versus, say, living in Montana, which also seems to have influenced your work?

Bottoms: We have a rich literary heritage in the South, but it's sometimes been at odds with the rest of the country. I didn't really understand the depth of this until I moved out of the South for a while. I first began to glimpse how other folks look at us a few years ago when I did a reading at Columbia. It was at a symposium on Southern poetry sponsored by the Academy of American Poets, and I was up there with Charles Wright and Robert Morgan. We had a good audience and they were very receptive. I mean the place was packed. I don't remember any specific questions anyone asked, but there was generally a sort of *Tobacco Road* curiosity. Also, when I lived in Montana I discovered that folks in some parts of the country don't care very much for the South. Given our history this is understandable, I suppose. My wife was very prejudiced against Southerners. She had this terrible notion that all Southern men were misogynists and all Southern women were bimbos. So there are certain liabilities that come with being from the South. We're still regarded as cultural primitives. This is a misconception, of course. Nevertheless, it's still alive and thriving in many parts of the country. Still, the South is a fascinating place. We have a culture that's still fairly unique. Wasn't it Faulkner who said the past isn't dead, it's not even the past? I live about a mile and a half from a Civil War battlefield, so I move through a piece of history just about every day.

Browning: What about the poems? How does living in the South affect your poetry?

Bottoms: Well, the history and the culture obviously enter the poems, but I think the South has a unique feel about it also. The landscape, the animals, the trees, all give it a special feel. And the relationship of the people to the land. And the importance of religion. Even our relationship to guns. All of these things are connected. In fact, I think "Shooting Rats" could've only been written in the South.

Browning: Did Montana have a special feel too?

Bottoms: Absolutely. Most places do, I suppose, once you get out of sight of the Golden arches, the Burger Kings, and the Pizza Huts. But yes, Montana has a very strong and individual feel for me. First of all, the landscape is amazing. The open spaces are overwhelming, and they make you feel totally insignificant. And the wildlife, is of course, very different from the wildlife in the South. You don't feel a great sense of history there, but you feel a much greater intimacy with the wilderness. They have grizzlies and mountain lions, so the woods can be dangerous. And so can the winters. But living there for a couple of years was very good for me. I got a new perspective on my life and on my poems. I had a new country to work with.

Limehouse: When you were talking a little bit earlier about the South as a place, the traditions, and using this as material, a phrase came into my head—"a sense of sin."

Bottoms: Well, we live in the Bible belt.

Limehouse: But maybe sin also has to do with racial issues, and maybe with the whole Faulknerian family stuff, and maybe somehow with the density of the landscape, with the land being almost too green, too lush.

Bottoms: I don't know how much of that I feel personally. Probably not much. Certainly, I don't feel any racial guilt, though I feel the cultural burden of that, which is a different thing. Someone asked me in an interview once why I didn't write about racial issues. My response was something like "Wouldn't it be great to write *To Kill a Mockingbird*?" But Harper Lee already did that, and I don't believe I could top it.

Limehouse: Talking about the Bible belt brings up something else. You use a lot of religious imagery—*In a U-Haul North of Damascus*, *Any Cold Jordan*, *Easter Weekend*.

Bottoms: Yes, I was raised in the Baptist Church. And I'm a Christian, if a somewhat loose and strange one. Anyway, that's my religion and my culture, so that's a natural bag of images. If I were a Buddhist the images would be different.

Limehouse: Of course, you're not going to find that in the average *New Yorker* poem.

Bottoms: No, you're not. Which is neither here nor there in terms of the poetry. But it may be a comment about the country we live in. Our culture is fairly secular, and I don't much like that. I appreciate the mystery. And that's another thing I believe good poems should do, they should define the mystery for us. Not solve it, of course, which is impossible. But they should teach us the right questions to ask.

Browning: What about religious music? I know you love gospel music. Do you think there is any connection between religious music and the sound in your poems?

Bottoms: Well, I think most Southern writers are influenced by the music of the King James Bible, but beyond that it gets very fuzzy. I think about sound when I write, of course, but mostly I've just learned over the years to trust my ear. I'm sure my sound in the poems is affected in some way by music but I can't really explain how.

Limehouse: Does trusting yourself as a poet get easier?

Bottoms: It does. But I don't know if that's good or bad. I think as I've gotten older that I spend less time at the typewriter trying to work out ideas. And twenty years ago I had the fire. I'd write a poem one afternoon and get it out in the mail the next morning. I'd keep 15 batches of things out in the mail. Otherwise I thought I was a failure. And if I didn't write constantly, I was a failure. One thing that's happened over the years is I've learned to do more editing in my head. I've learned what's going to work and what's not, so I don't beat myself up. I trust this sort of internal editor to tell me whether I need to go to the typewriter.

Limehouse: I was just thinking of a passage from Auden's *The Dyer's Hand*. He talks about a poet only knowing that he or she is a poet at the moment of finishing a poem. Up until that moment they were someone who was about to write a poem, and after that moment they are someone has written a poem and may never write one again. Can you speak to that?

Bottoms: That's true, in a sense, I suppose. When you know you're writing a good poem, you don't want to let it go. You don't want the whole creative process to end. It's euphoric. Another thing that's happened to me over the years is that I've learned to take a lot longer with a poem. I sort of relish the whole business of tuning it up. It's nothing now to tune one for months.

Limehouse: You wouldn't have done that when you were young?

Bottoms: No, not enough patience. And I felt a terrific urgency to publish then that I just don't feel anymore. Now I'd rather get it right before I send it out.

Limehouse: Is that a function of maturity?

Bottoms: It's a function of understanding that you're never going to be rich anyway. Or famous. Or if you think you're famous, you'll never be famous enough. And what does all that account for really? I think it's just a matter of settling down and understanding what's really important—and that's simply making the poem as solid as it can be.

Limehouse: That leads to another question. How has having a child affected your work or your perception of your work?

Bottoms: It's changed my perspective dramatically. I'm not the center of my universe anymore. I used to think the story of creation ended with me, and I was put here to write about it. All writers have this sort of ego, I think, or at least begin this way. But a child in your family makes you understand how really unimportant your life is. If I had my choice of being a great writer or a great father, I'd always opt for the latter. Also, having a daughter rather than a son has been a very interesting education for me. It's made me much more aware of the ways our culture discriminates against women. It's made me aware of a lot of ugliness that I'd never noticed before and perhaps had even participated in. In short, I'd say that my daughter has made me a better person, and also, perhaps, a better writer.

FISHING FROM THE POETRY BOAT:
A Conversation with
Alice Friman and Bruce Gentry

This interview was conducted on two occasions, initially after a reading in the Allen and Helen Kellogg Writers Series at the University of Indianapolis, shortly after the 1995 release of *Armored Hearts: Selected and New Poems*, and again in 1997 at the South Central Modern Language Association meeting in Dallas.

Friman: I notice that the "I" in many of your poems, especially in *Under the Vulture-Tree*, seems to be a hero, one who saves, a sort of knight errant. Is that true?

Bottoms: I've never thought much about myself as a hero, but maybe that voice comes out of the whole notion of redemption, that things can be salvaged, saved. That's always been a very compelling notion to me. You could probably trace it fairly easily through each of the books.

Friman: I'd like for us to talk about *Under the Vulture-Tree* awhile because I love that book, I've lived with it, and sometimes when I'm having difficulty doing something technically in my own work, I look to that book to teach me.

Bottoms: You're kidding.

Friman: I do. I say Bottoms, how did you do this? One of the things that comes through so strongly in *Vulture-Tree* is the character of the "I." You said in a 1991 interview with Eddie Lee Rider that you're not the same person who wrote those poems. I want to know who was the person who wrote *Vulture-Tree*? How is he different from the "I" who wrote the new poems in *Armored Hearts*?

Bottoms: That's not a difficult distinction. The *Vulture-Tree* book was written when I lived in east Cobb County on a little pond. I was married to my first wife then, and things were relatively calm in my life. I spent a lot of time fishing and playing guitar. I was teaching at Georgia State. I had come a few years earlier from Florida. I can't remember if there are any Florida poems in that book or not. Well, the title poem. Anyway, I was in a fairly good place in my life. Or so it seemed. "White Shrouds" came out of that house and "In the Ice Pasture." And "Ice" and "Red Swan" and "The Voice of Wives Dreaming." It was a period of relative peace and ease just before I went to University of Montana to be the Hugo Poet-in-Residence. Montana, certainly, was a turning point, personally and professionally, because it opened up a whole new landscape. I went out there to teach, and my wife stayed home in Georgia. We'd been growing more distant for several years, and we didn't really have much in common anymore, although there was no animosity.

We'd gotten married when we were very young, and when I came back from Montana, we decided to part ways.

Friman: How long were you in Montana?

Bottoms: I was only there for one term that time. Then I came home to Georgia and went through the divorce. I'd met a woman up there, Kelly, and as you know we later married. She was in law school at the University of Montana, and so we had a long-distance relationship for about a year. I'd just gotten several grants, and I think I spent most all of the money on airline tickets. After the divorce and a year of living the long-distance relationship, I took a year off from Georgia State and moved to Billings to finish *Easter Weekend*. Kelly had moved there to start a law practice. Consequently, the novel has all that Montana business in it.

Friman: You said *Vulture-Tree* is from that time of relative peace before everything sort of shredded apart.

Bottoms: Peter Davison told me once—he'd stayed with us in that house—that he was very sorry I'd lost that place because he knew it was really important to my poems. It hadn't really occurred to me how many of the poems came out of that house and pond but a lot of them did. Fortunately, Montana was a good place too. It was so open, a totally new landscape. The poems, when I got to Montana, opened up a little bit also, so that many of them ceased to have the hard closure that characterizes most of my other poems. That vastness of landscape, I think, was very good for me. In a place like that you feel almost immediately this great sense of possibility.

Friman: I notice in the *Shooting Rats* poems, especially "Watching Gators at Ray Boone's Reptile Farm," there are various themes that run through the complete *Armored Hearts*. One of these is the idea of a common memory—what you call the "breathable past." I know you talk frequently in your classes about the concepts of Carl Jung. Did you mean this in any Jungian sense?

Bottoms: No, I had something different in mind here. I do talk a lot in my workshops about archetypes, about Jung's notion of racial memory, which I really find fascinating. But those particular poems came out of an interesting idea I got from Carl Sagan—I forget who actually pioneered this particular research, but Sagan distilled it for the common guy in his *Dragons of Eden*. It was the notion of the triune brain, that the brain actually developed as three different brains, all of which are still there. The first is that little mass of tissue at the top of the spine, the R Complex or the reptile brain, which supposedly controls eating, sex, and ritual, and then on top of that the limbic or mammal brain, which controls emotion, and finally on top of that the neo-cortex, huge in comparison, which supposedly accounts for abstract thought and differentiates us from other creatures, which I believe isn't quite thought to be true anymore. Aren't they figuring out that apes actually abstract in some small way? At any rate, that's where those things come from—the notion of the reptile brain, the triune brain. Sort of the lowest common denominator, the biological link. I suppose I've always been drawn toward those primitive aspects of the psyche.

Gentry: Aren't you still sometimes writing out of that?

Bottoms: Oh, absolutely. It runs through all poems. It runs through "U-Haul," "Vulture-Tree," "Armored Hearts," all the animal poems. I think I still have the same notions about how that affects our relationships. The most important aspect, of course, is how it connects us with the world, the wilderness. That's our last remnant of wildness, our last little bit of the primordial.

Friman: And for you the animal world is what?

Bottoms: The animal world is the real world. To me the world out there in the woods is the real world, the world the way it was made, and everything else is something of an aberration, much less significant. Indeed, in some cases such as cyberspace, actually obscene and dehumanizing. Nature is always right. The very best poets have always understood this. It's a notion, of course, that's fundamental to the romantic movement. Actually, it's just plain fundamental. I'm still very attracted to the tenets Wordsworth set down in his famous preface, especially to his observations concerning what he calls "the low and rustic life." This is not a macho thing in the *Deliverance* sense, but a heartfelt notion that one can actually be more comfortable and "natural," if you will, living a less complicated sort of life. This is what I aspired to but have not been able to accomplish.

Friman: And what would that require?

Bottoms: What I'd really like to do now is move to the woods, get a little piece of land out in the boonies. Something in me keeps leaning out toward the trees. That's my big dream.

It's the old reptile brain, of course. If we give it half a chance, it'll recognize something out there, remember, and sway out toward it. I still catch it trying to make those connections. Like that old poem "The Copperhead" where something in the persona, some fascination or affinity, keeps pulling him down into the water and toward the snake.

Friman: I'd like for you to talk about the technique you use when dealing with the past in poems like "The Voice of Wives Dreaming," "The Desk," "The Anniversary," and "In Louisiana." It's as if you evoke the past so that it's suddenly called up into a vivid present. You never say "I remember." You change tenses, you say "I see it." And it begins to happen like a vision, so the reader sees vividly what you're seeing in your memory.

Gentry: So it's more vivid than the present.

Friman: It *is* the present, the past taking over.

Bottoms: That's interesting, but I don't think about that. It may all be related in some peripheral way to the act of narrative itself. Narration is often the past made immediate, it's just storytelling, of course, and the importance of detail is to make the world alive again on the page. It's a matter of being convincing. I really believe that all readers are basically skeptics, and your first obligation as a writer is to overcome that skepticism. You can only do that with convincing detail, to make readers willingly fling away that disbelief, at least for the period of time they're involved with the poem. That's Coleridge's phrase, isn't it? The "willing suspension of disbelief." He talks about it in *Biographia Literaria*. Anyway, verb tense for the sake of immediacy or anything else is only a narrative technique, one of many things you use to convince the reader of your veracity. I like something the poet Karl Shapiro said in an essay called "What Is Not Poetry." He said, "If poetry has an opposite, it is philosophy. Poetry is a materialization of experience; philosophy is the abstraction of it." That crystallizes, I think, the challenge the poet faces, especially a narrative poet. Your business is to make the world physical on the page. And this is, at least partly, an act of imaginative re-creation.

Friman: In the poem "In a Kitchen, Late," you speak of "making yourself no presence in the room." Would you talk about the importance of passivity or negative capability?

Bottoms: That poem is essentially about making yourself no human presence. Jane Hirshfield talks about something similar as a fundamental approach in poetry, the notion of developing a particular mind-set or attitude in which the self disappears so that the deeply shy aspects of the landscape can emerge. I like that. It's pretty much the same thing Faulkner is talking about in his bear story when Sam Fathers tells the boy if he wants to see Old Ben he'll have to leave his rifle and watch behind. In the "Kitchen" poem, this also has to do with trying to re-enter the wilderness, the roaches are bringing a little bit of it back to you. Still, it's impossible for you really to accomplish that—face it, you like your nice house in the suburbs. And more to the point, you're self-conscious, you rationalize. Any creature that is self-conscious can't ever totally regain the instinctive impulse that governs the life of animals. James Dickey probably has the best poem in the language about this whole question. It's called "The Sheep Child." Jim told me once that he didn't care what anybody said about that poem, he didn't think it could be faulted for originality of point of view. Well, that's what the poem's all about, right? It has some great lines: "I saw for a blazing moment/ The great grassy world from both sides,/ Man and beast in the round of their need,/ And the hill wind stirred in my wool,/ My hoof and my hand clasped each other." Here's one of the fundamental questions of human existence, this great feeling we have of being displaced from the natural world by virtue of our own self-consciousness. This is the whole story of the Fall, isn't it? And here he unites these two aspects again—the rational and the instinctive—in the point-of-view of this sheep child, and of course the irony is that this is so horribly unnatural the sheep child dies immediately. What a great line, "My hoof and my hand clasped each other." Anyway, I think that's the whole notion of making yourself "no presence in the room." It's an attempt—feeble as it might be—to experience that reunification to whatever degree you can accomplish it, which probably isn't very much.

Friman: In light of that, how do the jon boat and water fit in?

Bottoms: Water is a medium into the natural world, that's all. The jon boat is a mode of transportation. The act of fishing itself is really fascinating to me, emotionally and psychologically. I talk about poetry a lot in terms of fishing.

Friman: Like Thoreau?

Bottoms: Well, fishing is a great metaphor for poetry, if you think about it, at least for the way I look at poetry. My kind of poetry is this constant dredging up of things out of the psyche, poetry as self-exploration that reveals the contours of the general. I like what Seamus Heaney says in an essay called "Feeling into Words." The first time he ever wrote what he thought was a good poem, he says, he felt like he'd let down a shaft of light into himself. Poetry, the act of creation, had become an act of self-discovery. I feel the same way, and fishing is an interesting metaphor for the process. You're out there alone in the little poetry boat, throwing out your lure—a good word here—and you're casting down into the depths, the psychic depths. Of course, you're going for the creative impulse, the stuff of the great poem, you're going for the seven-pound bass, but you don't know what's down there. You just have to be willing to cast out that Jitterbug or that Mirr-O-Lure and take whatever hits the line. All of this ties into an idea Carl Jung had about creativity. I believe he talked about this in relation to manic-depressive illness. Ironically, the seeds of creativity are mixed into what Jung calls the "slime from the depth," that psychic slime, the ugliest and most animalistic aspects of our personality. These are all those fearful things we've confined, repressed into our unconscious. But if you're after the creative impulse, you have to be willing to wallow around in that a little bit. Or coming back to the metaphor, you have to be willing to drag up whatever hits your lure—gar, copperhead, water mocassin, alligator. All of this for me—the water, the jon boat, the fishing—is a way of talking about the process of discovering the poem.

Friman: Why do you call the entire new and selected poems *Armored Hearts*?

Bottoms: "Armored Hearts" is one of the earlier poems in the last section of that book, the new poems, and it just sort of kept coming up at readings. The title suggests several things to me. Of course, it refers to turtles and that armament they have, but it also refers to a kind of a self-defensive mechanism I think that we all learn to build early on in our lives. In some ways, living in our culture, requires an armored heart. I talk a good bit to my students about the creative process, about where ideas come from, and all I've ever figured out is that the writer must simply be as sensitive to the world as he or she can stand, hoping that an idea hits. But sensitivity is a hazardous thing too. The world can be overwhelming. All hearts have a kind of armament that we construct to protect ourselves from the onslaught. Otherwise, the grief would squash us. The trick is finding that fine line, absorbing every impulse you can from the world without overburdening yourself, without getting squashed.

Friman: In the poem "Armored Hearts" the two human characters seem like the two sides of yourself—the one who saves things, the ducks here (going back to David Bottoms as knight), and the other one, a darker one, like the turtles themselves, clinging to solitude.

Bottoms: Actually both men in the poem are saving things. One is trying to save the ducks, the other the turtles. I guess I'm drawn more to the turtles. They're that sort of submerged aspect of the personality, the secretive—I might even say the mysterious, the hidden, the almost mystical aspect of one's personality, one's psyche, much more primitive than the ducks. The ducks are creatures of the surface. They fly, they're airy. Yes, I'd side with the turtles. So the persona goes out at the end of the poem and strips the bait off the hooks of the guy who's trying to catch them.

Gentry: I want to ask the question over again. Don't you think that there's some of you in the guy with the pistol?

Bottoms: Trying to shoot the turtles?

Gentry: Yes. I say that because of the way you introduce the poem at readings, the way you set it up, making the guy trying to save the ducks sound so sympathetic. Everybody in the room who hasn't read the poem expects you to side with the savior of ducks—then they are given a big shock when you read the end of the poem. When I hear you introduce the poem, I think this question makes sense.

Bottoms: Maybe that's the social aspect of the personality—getting along with our neighbors—oh yes, of course—oh, the turtles are killing the ducks, how horrible, of course you've got to go get those turtles. But then the other aspect emerges and dominates. And essentially it becomes dominant at night, doesn't it? In secret. He goes out at night and strips away the bait.

Gentry: We were theorizing that when you put that title on the book you were saying that with these new poems, "I'm going to show you my turtle side a little bit more than I have in the past."

Friman: To me the "I" in your newer poems is different than in the rest of the book, the selected poems, because of that. I think the poems in the "Armored Hearts" section are much darker.

Bottoms: I might agree with that. As I said, I went through a divorce when I was 37 or 38. That was a terrible thing, though it was not a messy legal business as some divorces are. I'd been married for 15 years and gotten very comfortable, then suddenly I had nothing. I think I left that marriage with about $1000 and a truck. I just gave it all away, house, bank account, everything. So I was asking a lot of questions about my life and where I was going, and frankly the next few years were quite a struggle.

Friman: So all of these new poems came from those years?

Bottoms: Yes, and then on top of all that every word I'd ever written went out of print. All those books that Morrow published sold pretty well for poetry—about five thousand copies each, the editions all sold out—but they didn't reprint them. It was really disheartening. But this isn't an uncommon thing for American poets. You hear horror stories all the time, all of which makes me very grateful to the folks at Copper Canyon for taking me on. Sam Hamill has been able to build an excellent press out there because he cares deeply about poetry and poets know that.

Gentry: Is a good editor essential for a poet? You've said that you'd published all these books with Morrow and you couldn't get your editor on the phone.

Bottoms: A good editor is essential for any writer who wants to publish a book. And yes, that's right. In my seven or so years at Morrow I could hardly even get my editor to return a phone call. So I'm spending my whole life writing poems and I'm wondering why I'm doing this. Why am I beating my brains out doing this? Obviously, the only good reason to write poems is because you enjoy it. You certainly don't do it for the money or the celebrity. Young writers sometimes have silly ideas about this. That's why I try to drill into them the dangers of false ambition. The only good ambition, of course, is to write something you like. But, yes, it was a difficult time in many ways, having worked so hard for so long and not even to have a book in print, not a novel or a book of poems, and about the only way to deal with that in the poetry was to write a poem like "Allatoona Evening." Then again, my vision has always been bleak. I do not have what Flannery O'Connor calls "a naturally sunny disposition."

Gentry: You've talked about the poet as an FM receiver.

Bottoms: Yes, that's one of my cornier metaphors for the poet. I think I was talking about the way we receive the poem, the engendering idea. And I was talking again about that Heaney essay, "Feeling into Words," where he describes the creative process as two separate stages. I like that. The first is that sort of initial idea or inspiration, maybe an image or a phrase, that first impulse that a poem needs to be written, and then the second stage is the craft of writing, taking that idea to the notebook, the typewriter, or the word processor, and fleshing out the original impulse, applying all that we've learned about poetry. Of course, this second stage can actually be facilitated. This is what we try to do in writing classes when we teach folks about figurative language, sound devices, narrative, myth. But the first the first stage—the initial impulse—which is the real creative act, is slightly more mysterious. There really doesn't seem to be very much you can teach anyone about that. Either it happens or it doesn't, the idea comes or it doesn't. The only thing anyone can do, I think, is to make himself or herself more available to the world, more receptive to things going on, and so the analogy of the radio receiver. The world is trying to send us these signals and we have to be tuned in. But, as I said earlier, that's a dangerous thing also, being that sensitive to the world is to open yourself up, to chip the armor off. Anyway, I simply preach the trick of living as close to the edge as you can, exercising as much sensitivity and receptivity as you can stand.

Gentry: I also want you to say something about the differences between writing poetry and fiction.

Bottoms: Well, for me about the only similarity is that I write them both in English. The essential difference, I suppose, is what each genre seeks to do with language. Fiction, of course, especially the novel, is the process of expansion, of fleshing out plot and characterization into some compelling story. Poetry is more the art of compression, the art of suggestion. Poetry requires much more of language because it's the art of making language work figuratively, making words suggest beyond their literal meanings in the context of the poem. And often, of course, it's the art of learning what not to say, the art of letting the silences do their own kind of talking. So there are really two different sensibilities at work here and they don't mix easily.

Gentry: Which for you is the more pleasurable work?

Bottoms: The poetry, by far. I'd much rather have the poetry than the fiction because I think poetry simply requires more of language. And the experience of writing it is so much more intense. Fiction writing is much more like a job. You get an idea for a piece of fiction, you sit down for a couple of weeks and plot it all out and you have something to work on from nine to five for the next two or three years. Poetry is much more a product of the inspired moment. Don't get the notion this is something that takes place in fifteen or twenty minutes, or even an hour or two. A first draft might take that long, but then the real work of revision comes. Still, even in revision it seems easier, at least for me, to catch again that original spark of excitement.

Friman: You sound like a poet who has no real discipline in his work habits.

Bottoms: That's right, and I think it's important not to. A lot of young poets sit down at their typewriters every morning and face that blank page without the foggiest idea driving them. They just have this need to create, this need to write. I empathize with that, but I think that's one of the worst forms of self-abuse a poet can practice. I never go to the typewriter unless I have a pretty clear grasp of some propelling idea, unless the world actually has suggested something interesting to me. And this is the problem with so many poems these days—they just don't have any sense of necessity about them. The real poem, the necessary poem, doesn't come often, and patience is something young writers usually have to learn the hard way.

Gentry: About the poem "Sign for My Father, Who Stressed the Bunt." We both thought you were talking about sacrifice in terms of the poet, what's required to be a poet. Do you buy that?

Bottoms: No, I think that's reading too much into the poem. You can certainly extend the notion of sacrifice to any of the arts, nothing worthy is accomplished without sacrifice and all that, but I don't think that poem was ever intended to be metaphor for art. The poem is about my father and about baseball. The sacrifice in its figurative sense is the sacrifice of one generation for the next.

Gentry: Well, I was going to say that "Under the Boathouse" seems like another poem very much about writing. You don't think so? I mean, the naked man jumping head first into the lake he knows nothing about?

Bottoms: I don't know. I suppose you might read that as a metaphor for the creative act, the willingness to dive in. We were talking about fishing as a metaphor for poetry and that's the same sort of thing. But I wasn't thinking about that. One thing, though, that I do find interesting about "Under the Boathouse" is the way it works figuratively. I spend a lot of time with students talking about narrative, but I'm careful to warn them that narrative isn't all you need to make a good poem. Actually, not nearly enough. For me, at least, much of the art of poetry is the way it works figuratively, the way it suggests something beyond itself. The poem needs to spring from that concrete situation or narrative context into what we call the DHM, the Deep Hidden Meaning. Usually this happens through language, but oddly enough, there is at least one other way this can happen. That's when the narrative itself becomes figurative, when it touches archetypal pattern and myth. This is what I was going for in "Under the Boathouse." In the elements of the narrative it mirrors what Jung calls the "myth of the night journey," the submersion, the symbolic death, ascension and rebirth he saw illustrated in the Old Testament story of Jonah and the whale. This is, of course, a pattern that repeats itself constantly in the literature of virtually all cultures. Most students are fairly quick to recognize the elements of baptism. And they're right. The poem is literally about a man diving into a lake, but the narrative pattern resonates in the reader in ways that he or she may not immediately recognize.

Gentry: Do you think about things like that when you are writing?

Bottoms: Yes, certainly. If you look at the language in that poem, you'll see that when the persona of the poem is surfacing, ascending, he looks up and he sees the shadow of his wife on top of the water, like an angel in a dead man's float. And he makes references to heavenly litter, things like that. So the language in the poem tries to reinforce the archetypal pattern.

Gentry: In *Any Cold Jordan* there seems to be a connection between music and crime. Sometimes I think you might relate writing and crime. Is that right? Any connection to the poetry? You say your writing is all autobiographical, after all, and both of the novels are heading toward crime with a lot of their energy.

Bottoms: That's an interesting question. I haven't really thought about that, but the poem "The Desk" comes immediately to mind.

Gentry: Yes. And the one where you are about to steal a car for somebody.

Bottoms: "In the Black Camaro." Also "Rendezvous: Belle Glade" and "Light of the Sacred Harp." And "Wrestling Angels," an even older poem, which is about a graveyard vandal. It probably has more to do with the notion of authority, don't you think? And the notion that we all have these impulses in our lives, these notions that we as individuals are really more significant than any imposed authority. I mean that we have more moral authority, that our needs and rights account for more morally than the authority held by the Cherokee County Board of Education or the Indianapolis City Council, or the Police Department, or the Constitution of the United States. Who are these people who keep forcing us to live by their rules? Well, in art we can explore these things. My agent, Maria Carvainis, has a great line. She's an incredibly perceptive reader, as you might expect, and she's sort of condensed the art of fiction into one sentence: "All good fiction is about the right to sin." There's a lot in that—the whole conflict between legal authority and moral authority, which can lead to a kind of justifiable sin and justifiable rebellion.

Friman: That's certainly true in the poem "The Desk."

Bottoms: Yes. The persona just says to himself, "This desk really belongs to me. I'm just going to go on up there and get it." And he goes up to the old school building at one o'clock or so in the morning with a crowbar and a hammer, and he breaks in.

Friman: Of course, he does make it very clear that he's never done this before, thus maintaining his "goodness."

Gentry: In *Any Cold Jordan*, the Jerry Lamberti character seems to be a symbol of the danger of being ruined by artistic integrity, the absolute refusal to sell out. Do you think of your art in terms of high and low, integrity and selling out?

Bottoms: I don't know. If I had an idea for a book that I knew would sell like *The Bridges of Madison County*, I'd certainly be tempted to write it. But I don't seem to have much talent for touching the popular taste. Whatever flaws my two novels have, I think they were both written primarily from an artistic impulse. I really feel like *Easter Weekend* has an interesting sort of mythic underpinning, with the open grave and the Easter business. The book came to me the same way that poems tend to come—with that sort of initial flash of an idea. And it was all there, as a whole. I don't feel as if I really compromised very much. I didn't write it to please a large audience, I wrote it the way I wanted it. Two screenplays have been done, and both give it a happy-ever-after ending. That's what you expect from Hollywood, and I've never been very interested in Hollywood. The only thing those guys care about is what sells. But I am interested in talking about Jerry Lamberti. He's based on a friend of mine who's a blues musician, an incredible musician but mostly a kind of acoustic blues guitarist, a Josh White or Big Bill Broonsy type. He's spent thirty years of his life living in real poverty in Macon, Georgia, because there's just no commercial market for that kind of music. I have some respect for that. And that's really the same question that Billy Parker has to deal with. He's most happy with his music when he's playing what he enjoys and feels he has some sort of artistic integrity. His problem is simple, at this point in his life he needs some commercial success. But in order to achieve that kind of success he has to compromise, he has to sing the hokey country songs the drunks in the bars want to hear.

Gentry: So what about the jon boat business, what about Billy's passivity? Is this a copout, a sign of his failure?

Bottoms: Well, there are different kinds of success, aren't there? When he's out there fishing, just floating alone on the water, trying to become a part of it all out in the wilderness, or when he's playing his own music, he's very close to the voice in many of my poems, to the aesthetic of something like "Allatoona Evening." This is a different sort of ambition. And really the only one that counts. The sort of integrity and peace he finds out there accounts for little in the real world, the world of the American greenback, but it accounts for a lot on a personal level.

Gentry: But as you say, there is the real world to think about. Jerry has to go out and get a job because he's not making enough with his art. And he hurts his hand so he's not quite as able to play. It's as if the book is saying you need to sell out to an audience just a little bit and then you'll be all right. Who is your audience, and is it different for the poetry than for the fiction?

Bottoms: I don't really visualize any particular audience. I think I just try to say things as best as I can, as though I were writing for any literate and intelligent person. I remember reading somewhere that someone, maybe Peter Stitt, editor of *The Gettysburg Review*, asked Robert Penn Warren "How do you read a poem?" and Warren thought for a minute and said, "Slowly." I think that says what I really feel about audience. Anyone who will take the time and really give the poem the consideration it deserves is my audience.

Gentry: Do you have people you show your poems to?

Bottoms: Yes, I've always found that helpful, but I don't show them to many people. When I was in college I didn't have access to any creative writing workshops, which was probably a blessing, but there were a couple of professors I felt comfortable showing things to. This worked well enough, and at different places in my life I've been lucky enough to find a good reader here and there. Occasionally I send things to Dave Smith, who's a good friend, and he's very helpful. But over the last ten years or so the only person I've shown poems to on a regular basis is Bob Hill. Bob has done some fine work on Dickey, and he's an excellent reader. Also, he's a close and good friend, which is essential, because only a close friend will tell you the truth. So I'll work on a poem for a few weeks until I've done about all I can do for a while, then I'll pick up the phone and say, "Bob, I'm faxing something over." If he has any problems with it, I'll just go back to work.

Gentry: Whenever you talk about *Easter Weekend* you say something about religion. Would you compare how religion comes into that novel with how religion comes into the poetry?

Bottoms: Religion in *Easter Weekend* is only kind of a underpinning that tries to gives the book some mythic depth. We see these characters moving across a landscape and we recognize certain archetypes operating, and this opens up a few possibilities for irony. Will Connie be resurrected? Questions like that. In the poems religion is much more personal and substantial, important in a more direct way, I think. The poems draw on it and wrestle with it in ways the fiction has yet to attempt. It's fundamental to the poems, but still peripheral to the novels.

Gentry: Would you talk about the St. Augustine epigraph to *Armored Hearts*? What does that do for the book? What does that say about you?

Bottoms: I was reading St. Augustine's *Confessions* and that passage just jumped out at me, and I marked it. When I was putting *Armored Hearts* together, I remembered it. Then I looked at three or four different translations. The one I used is by far the least literal, but the most beautiful, and I felt guilty about that. So I asked a friend of mine, Bill Sessions, who's a Renaissance scholar and has good Latin, and he chose this one also. "My soul is like a house," Augustine says. Maybe I meant to suggest that the book is also like a house, a place where the soul expresses itself. The book reflects what's working in the soul, and it's not all nice stuff. All is not sunlight and flowers. There are dark thoughts. "It is in ruins," he says. And I think that's particularly apt to the latter part of the book. And then he says, "but I ask you to remake it."

Gentry: Yes, that's the line that gets me. What are you asking me to do?

Bottoms: I'm not asking you to do anything. St. Augustine was talking to God. Only God can put some order there.

Gentry: Are you religious then?

Bottoms: Yes, though that requires some explanation and for a long time I felt odd about discussing it. In these days of the religious right, if you say you believe in God, in a creating spirit, many folks are apt to think you're unsophisticated, if not a little simple. This attitude seems arrogant to me. There's an intelligence of the head and an intelligence of the heart. But to answer your question, I was raised Southern Baptist, and though it's meant less to me at various times in my life, I think that over the last ten or so years Christianity has become very important. I don't go to church regularly, and I think most Christian churches today are a far cry from the early church Paul founded, nevertheless I call myself a Christian.

Actually, I feel a good deal of empathy with Reynolds Price when he calls himself an "outlaw Christian." I just finished reading his *Three Gospels*, which is a book of very literal translations of the gospels of Mark and John, as well as an apocryphal gospel of his own. The translations are fascinating, but the essays introducing them are even better. Somewhere in one of those essays he sets down his own very interesting statement of faith. I don't remember precisely the argument he makes, but one phrase has stuck. He says that Jesus of Nazareth seems to have stood in "a demonstrably but inexplicably intimate relation to the creator." And he goes on to say that the intensity of this relationship, to his knowledge, is unique in human history, unique to the point of demonstrating some degree of identity between Jesus and God. That's well said, I think. Beyond that what we can believe about the historical Jesus is a matter of great debate, though Reynolds seems to invest a good deal of confidence into the authority of the canonical gospels, especially Mark and John, as do I.

Gentry: So when you read this epigraph, it's like a prayer.

Bottoms: It's St. Augustine's prayer, and I find it meaningful. He talks about perfection as being a kind of evolution, of God remaking his life, not instantaneously, but a gradual sort of working toward perfection. And I think what the poems are trying to do, especially in the last half of *Armored Hearts*, is find a gradual sort of path toward resignation and peace. Christianity provides that in a way, through a shedding of false ambition, which just creates in us anger and frustration.

Gentry: Sounds like you're putting a lot of emphasis on the last poem in the book, "Allatoona Evening."

Bottoms: Yes, that's a very important poem for me in a number of ways. It's a poem that came out of many frustrations—about writing and teaching and a lot of other things—and I think the key lines of the poem are about this equating of anger and ambition, where it talks about the bats and the whippoorwills and the copperheads and everything out there by the lake saying "lay it down," lay it all down. They say "your ambition,/ which is only anger,/ which sated could bring you to no better place." Even if all our ambitions were fulfilled, they could bring us to no better spiritual place than this one moment here beside this lake with "these three stars soaking up twilight." I really like the ending of that poem.

Gentry: So what would you say is a healthy kind of ambition?

Bottoms: For a poet, the healthiest kind of ambition is simply to want to write the best poem you can write and leave it at that, regardless of what happens to be the current taste at *The New Yorker* or *The Paris Review*. Who cares? All you're trying to do is write the very best poem you can write, and figure out how that illuminates and deepens the sense of meaning in your own life. Whatever happens or doesn't happen for you professionally, you'll always have your poems. And in your writing life that's the only thing that's important—you and your relationship to your words. If you're honest with yourself and follow your own impulses, that's something you can keep as a joy.

THE ONION'S DARK CORE:
A Conversation with Ernest Suarez

This conversation was taped in the spring of 1997, primarily in a pickup truck on I-75 between Atlanta and Macon, Georgia. Suarez was doing work on the relationship between rock music and poetry, and was in Georgia researching the Allman Brothers Band.

Suarez: You won the Walt Whitman Award in 1979. What were you doing then?

Bottoms: I'd been teaching high school for four or five years in Douglas County, Georgia. It hadn't been a good situation, and I was thinking about going back to school to work on a doctorate. Also, for several years I'd been writing poems and trying to place them in the magazines. I'd racked up around sixty since 1973 when I finished my MA—some in pretty good places such as *Harper's* and *Poetry*—and I'd chosen the best thirty or so and put together a manuscript. I sent it around to a few university presses, the University of Georgia Press and LSU, and it was rejected. Then a friend of mine, Gerald Duff, phoned and told me about the Walt Whitman Award, which is a first book competition sponsored by The Academy of American Poets. He suggested that I submit my book because Robert Penn Warren was the judge that year. I thought it would be great if Warren just read my poems. I fiddled with it some and changed the title to *Shooting Rats at the Bibb County Dump*, after a poem that had appeared in *Harper's*—the original title was *All Systems Break Down*—and I sent it off. A few months later I got a phone call from a very nice lady, Mrs. Marie Bullock. She introduced herself as the president of The Academy of American Poets and asked if I was sitting down. I said, "No ma'am, but I can sit down." And I did—on the side of the bed, as I recall. Then she said that Robert Penn Warren had chosen my book as winner of the Whitman Award. I was literally stunned with elation. I really don't remember anything else about the call. Later on Warren wrote me a nice note about the book. He also wrote a very generous comment for the jacket. It was a hard decision for him, I think. There were several good entries, and well over 1300 in all.

Suarez: And Morrow published it the following year?

Bottoms: Yes. At that time the Whitman book rotated between four publishers. It was William Morrow's year. I was very excited about having a first book, an award, and a New York publisher. The award included a $1000 cash prize. I don't think Warren really knew what all of that meant to me at the time. The real prize was the boost it gave me out of my situation. I was unhappy with my life and in a rut I feared would only get deeper. On the strength of the prize and a first book I was offered a fellowship to pursue my doctorate at Florida State, which is what I did.

Suarez: Is the manuscript that won the Whitman Award essentially the same as *Shooting Rats at the Bibb County Dump*?

Bottoms: Yes. There were a few minor changes. I added a poem called "The Copperhead," which had come out in *The Atlantic*. I asked Warren if I could include it, and he was agreeable, of course. I think I made a few minor changes to a couple of poems in the last section. Nothing serious. So it was basically the same book that Warren selected.

Suarez: Did you ever get to know Warren?

Bottoms: Not really, no. We only exchanged two or three letters, though he was very generous with young writers. I remember sending him a copy of a poem called "Under the Boathouse," and he made a good suggestion. But that's the only time I ever did anything like that. I didn't want to annoy him with a lot of correspondence I knew he didn't have time to answer. Later on, though, I did ask him for some poems when I was gathering a few for *Atlanta Magazine*, and he sent four or five good ones. "First Time" is the one I remember because I framed the signed manuscript and hung it in my office. Ironically, we only published one of the bunch before the whole staff was fired and I had to return them. A few months later a couple of them came out in *The New Yorker* and *The Georgia Review*.

Suarez: You never met?

Bottoms: No. I had two opportunities to meet him, but they both fell through. The first was in the early eighties at Bennington, where I was doing a reading. Dave Smith had arranged to drive me over to Warren's house, which was fairly close by, but as it turned out Warren was too sick. Several years later, Warren invited me to read at the Library of Congress. He was Poet Laureate then, the first actually. He was going to do the introduction, but he got sick again and couldn't travel. He sent his introduction along and one of the librarians read it. So I never got to meet him. That was a real disappointment.

Suarez: Go back to "Under the Boathouse." Do you recall the change that Warren suggested?

Bottoms: It had to do with point-of-view. The poem is about a fellow who dives into a pond and goes all the way down to the bottom where he gets his hand caught on a fish hook that's attached to something down there. Anyway, he's caught and can't tear loose, sort of hanging "Halfway between the bottom of the lake/ and the bottom of the sky." The line Warren suggested I change had to do with the moment when he's somewhat mysteriously freed. I'd written something like "In the lung-ache,/in the blue pulsing of temples," and he pointed out that the swimmer wouldn't be able to see his own temples. True enough, though I hadn't intended it exactly that way. Still, I didn't argue. I changed it to "loud pulsing of temples."

Suarez: You and James Dickey were friends for many years. He passed away recently. How would you assess his career and his significance to you as a poet?

Bottoms: I had a long phone conversation with Jim a few days before he died. He told me he was dying. He'd told me that before but this time I sensed it would be soon. He was very concerned with my opinion about his place in American poetry. I told him what I'd always told him. Simply that he was the champ. He liked the sports metaphor, and, as always, I said that with a clear conscience. He was a giant in American poetry. The attention he continues to draw will probably depend on the political fads of the critics, and you will have something to say about that. But from my perspective he was the finest poet to come out of the American South. His combination of narrative gift and lyricism seems to me unequalled. Others might argue for Warren, and they'd have some powerful ammo to shoot. Ultimately, it's probably a matter of sensibility and silly to weigh them against each other. They're both extraordinary. But Dickey's poetry, I think, has most influenced my own. His early work especially, and most especially in terms of the things he chose to write about. We had many of the same interests—fishing, hunting, bluegrass and old-time country music—and we came from the same part of the country. He showed me the poetic possibilities of the region we come from. But I don't think I write very much like Jim. Fred Chappell said once that in terms of style Dickey and I were just about as far apart as two writers could get. Dickey's power, he said, was expansion and mine was compression. I think that's a fair assessment. If you look at poems that are uniquely Dickey—say "The Firebombing,"

"Falling," "May Day Sermon," "The Zodiac"—you see that expansive imagination fiercely at work. It's almost as though the fullest degree of intensity must be wrung from each moment of the narrative. My best poems, I think—poems such as "Under the Vulture-Tree" or "White Shrouds"—tend to focus and compress the experience. My method, to me, seems closer to the method of James Wright in *The Branch Will Not Break*, which is still one of my favorite books. I'm thinking here of poems such as "A Blessing" or "A Dream of Burial." Or maybe to the Theodore Roethke of "The Meadow Mouse," "Slug," "The Pike." Ironically, though, what I really love of Roethke's is "The North American Sequence," which may be built out of a sensibility closer to Dickey's. I'm talking about that openness, that ability to touch every detail.

Suarez: But occasionally you've experimented with longer poems.

Bottoms: Yes, but my poems still tend to depend on focus and compression. If you look at *Armored Hearts*, you'll find very few poems that even run over 60 lines. And those are usually broken up into parts—for instance, "In a U-Haul North of Damascus." This is essentially a strategy for controlling the narrative, for reining it in, so I think Fred is probably right. Mine is ultimately a sensibility that leans toward compression, the illuminated moment. Though Dickey wrote some beautiful shorter poems—"The Performance," "Buckdancer's Choice," "Heaven of Animals," and I could go into a very long list—his imagination and lyric gift was such that he could sustain the intensity of the poem for pages.

My mind just doesn't work that way, and I may be fortunate that it doesn't. His talent simply dwarfed so many Southern poets, particularly those of his own generation.

Suarez: In what ways? Can you give us some specifics?

Bottoms: Well, it's not uncommon to hear Southern poets say that they've always felt like they were standing in Dickey's shadow. This is understandable. He threw a wide and tall one, and it must have been a dark place to find yourself. I remember hearing Van Brock, my old professor at Florida State, say that when he first started writing poetry his approach was very similar to Dickey's, but Dickey's voice was so powerful that he felt he had to alter his own. Now think about that. His natural inclination was to go at the poem much as Jim did, but Dickey did it so much better that he felt he had to change. This denial of one's own sensibility, one's own natural way of writing, has to be something like creative suicide. I remember hearing a musician friend of mine, a pianist, say that after she heard Horowitz in concert, she felt like going home and taking a hammer to her fingers. That was something like the effect Dickey's work had on other Southern poets.

Suarez: Let's push off that for a moment and talk about method. Can you describe what you try to accomplish in a poem?

Bottoms: In the introduction Warren wrote for the Library of Congress, he said that the world is always trying to tell us something. Or something to that effect.

Suarez: I'll read that to you. I have it here on the jacket of your *Vulture-Tree* book. He says, "Underlying all his work is the simple and unusual conviction that the world we see is trying to tell us something." What does he mean by that?

Bottoms: Simply that the world tries to tell us its secrets through the poem. The poem can reveal something about the hidden things of the world, the vague or shadowy relationships and connections that exist just below the surface of our daily lives. Or to say it another way, poetry can provide an artistic and emotional connection to the less obvious undercurrents of the world. I like that. I like to see poetry as a self-exploration of the personal that reveals through language the general patterns of human experience. I spend a lot of time in my classes discussing creativity and sensibility. I'm careful to tell my students that every writer who comes to class brings his or her own bag of prejudices. I have mine. Poetry, of course, means a lot of different things to different people, but for a long time I've been interested primarily in the way the poem works figuratively to reveal the universal through the personal. The meaning of the poem is always more than the sum of the literal meanings of all the words. We talk about the DHM—the deep hidden meaning— and how to get there through language. One element I emphasize from the start is narrative, what narrative can do for a poem simply because of what it is, simply because it carries with it so many of the basic elements of good writing. I like to use a little story about going out and buying a truck. A couple of years ago I bought a GMC pickup, and it didn't have a radio in it. Radios aren't standard equipment anymore. Well, that's a drag. Narrative in the poem is like buying a truck with everything on it. You get a package—radio, air conditioner, power windows, all at the same time. If you buy the narrative package you get a lot of good stuff. You at least get some degree of clarity, some sense of time and space. This is no small thing. It forces an attention to physical detail, the concrete, and so provides a greater sense of immediacy. It also provides what I call a concrete level of meaning, a narrative surface. Students always want their poems to be deep, and I say, "Well, in order to have a deeper meaning, you at least have to have one meaning for it to be deeper than. Right?" That's the narrative surface. In the narrative surface a good writer can embed various devices to spring the poem into the figurative, the DHM.

Suarez: And this is done through language?

Bottoms: Yes, through figurative devices. Metaphor, simile, word play, association, whatever. But oddly enough there's at least one other way this can happen, and that's when the narrative itself becomes figurative, when the narrative structure of the poem begins to mirror archetypal pattern and myth. I talk a good deal about Carl Jung's notions of archetype and the collective unconscious—this really fascinates me—and try to relate it to poetry. Take that poem "Under the Boathouse." As I said, this fellow jumps into a lake and goes all the way down to the bottom where he gets his hand caught on a hook and he can't get loose. He looks up and sees his wife's shadow floating on the surface "like an angel/ quivering in a dead-man's float." Then miraculously, he does tear loose and floats back up to the surface. So what you have mirrored here is simply an archetypal pattern—submersion, symbolical death, ascension, and rebirth. This pattern is what Jung calls the myth of the night journey, one of the oldest and most common patterns in Western culture. He cites as an example the Old Testament story of Jonah and the whale. We all know what happens there. God says to Jonah, "Go over here to Ninevah and preach to these bad people." And Jonah says to God, "Well, you know those people over there are mean, and they don't really like me. I was sort of thinking about taking a cruise." So Jonah tries to sail away from God, and the big storm comes up on the water. The crew treats Jonah to a swim, the big fish eats him, and he goes all the way down to the bottom of the sea, a symbolical death. Jonah begins to see then that Ninevah isn't such a terrible place after all. He has a change of heart. Then the great fish rises and spits him out on the other side, and he's a new Jonah. Descent, death, ascent, rebirth. That's just one of a number of narrative patterns that keep repeating themselves in the literatures of the world. Students are amazed when they're confronted with this, and soon enough they begin to see how the narrative structures of their own poems reverberate in odd ways because they bang up against archetypes.

Suarez: How much of this mirroring of the archetypal is a conscious part of the poet's strategy?

Bottoms: A good deal, I think. But fortunate things happen unconsciously too. Most everyone reading this will be familiar with Seamus Heaney's notion of the poem as dig, the poem as a type of personal archeology. He talks about this best in an essay called "Feeling into Words" where he says that the first time he ever wrote a poem he really liked, he felt as though he'd let a shaft of light down into himself. Well, the process of writing can produce some surprising and often intriguing discoveries. But the best thing that can happen for me is when the seed of the poem, the initial idea, is also the figurative device. I'll give you an example. When I was writing "Under the Vulture-Tree" the first line that came to me was the last line of the poem, "with mercy enough to consume us all and give us wings." I'd had a memory about an encounter with some vultures—on a fishing trip in north Florida—and I suddenly conceived of them as these "dwarfed transfiguring angels." An odd way to look at a vulture, but with it came the figurative device, the play on the words "consume" and "wings." The rest of the poem is simply a narrative architecture supporting that line. For me that one line is what makes the poem work. In "Sign for My Father, Who Stressed the Bunt" the same thing happened. The last line of the poem, "I'm getting a grip on the sacrifice," was the first to occur to me. The play on the word "sacrifice" in the dual contexts of a baseball game and a father's relationship to his son was the original idea for the poem. In my best poems, at least the shorter ones, this is what happens. The seed of the poem, the engendering idea, is the figurative device. About the worst thing that can happen is when I feel I want to write a poem about something and I don't have that device. I must have hundreds of drafts that are interesting narratives in themselves but fail to make that figurative leap, to reveal the connections operating under the surface. So I'm always careful to tell my students that as important as narrative is to poetry, it is not everything required to make a good poem. We're in a period now where narrative is hot again, perhaps as fashionable as the new formalism, but it can be equally as superficial. You can open up just about any magazine and find poems that are simply little stories broken up into twenty-five or thirty lines. They just lie there and never get beyond the literal. Perhaps this is why many poets—and some good Southern ones such as Ellen Voigt and Charles Wright—are suspicious of the narrative.

Suarez: Would you go back for a moment to "Under the Vulture-tree." I heard you say at a reading that it was typical of the way poems come to you. Could you describe in more detail how that poem came to be?

Bottoms: I was living in Tallahassee. This was around nineteen eighty or so, when I was doing my doctorate at FSU. One of my favorite pastimes was fishing, and there were some really beautiful rivers around Tallahassee. My favorite was the Wakulla. You'll know exactly what it looked like if I tell you that back in the forties two of those old Johnny Weissmuller Tarzan movies were made there, along with a movie called *The Creature from the Black Lagoon*. It was almost like a jungle, this slow tranquil river flowing through a jungle. Anyway, I was out there very early one morning, just about dawn, I think, and I was in a little aluminum boat. Then I came into a bend and on the far bank the jungle opened up into a small clearing. It was very odd because right in the middle of this clearing stood one giant black tree, so black you couldn't see light through it. It looked as though someone had taken a piece of black construction paper and cut out the silhouette of an oak tree and pasted it there. Well, it gave me a strange feeling so I drifted in a little closer. Then the strangeness intensified because I could see that it was a fruit tree. It was speckled all over with tiny pink fruit. As I got even closer the feeling turned eerie. These things weren't really fruit at all—they were heads, the heads of vultures. I'd come on a buzzard roost, and they were literally crammed into this tree shoulder to shoulder. Well, there's some material. Years later, maybe four or five, I was living in Marietta, Georgia, and something jarred that memory. As I said, for some reason the notion of these vultures as odd angels came to me and with that the word play on "consume" and "wings," which fell into the last line.

Suarez: Many of your poems are filled with wildlife. What's so important about animals?

Bottoms: Animals fascinate me because the real world is the wilderness. Everything else is artifice. By virtue of our consciousness we've separated ourselves from the natural world. No matter how many rivers we canoe down or how long we stay out in the woods, self-consciousness is still an act of separation. We've lost our instincts and must depend on our rational faculties. Few other people care much about this, but poets and other artists often feel intensely the need to get back to the some notion of the natural state. James Wright has his encounters with horses. James Dickey has his animals and violence. Think about that great poem "The Sheep Child." Talk about a unique point-of-view. In the wooly baby, the sheep child, Dickey achieves this amazing reunion of the two halves of human nature—the rational and the instinctive—and, of course, the irony lies in the fact that this is so horribly unnatural the sheep child dies immediately.

What a great line, "My hoof and my hand clasped each other."
Anyway, to put it simply, like many other poets I see animals
as a conduit into the real world. Several of my very early
poems deal with that. I'll give you an example. I've always
been fascinated with the notion of the triune brain, a concept
I ran across in a Carl Sagan book called *The Dragons of
Eden*. I forget who actually pioneered this research, but Sagan
distilled it for the common guy, a thing he was very good at
doing. Anyway, it's the concept that the brain actually
developed as three different brains, all of which are still
there. The first is that little mass of tissue at the top of the
spine, the R Complex or the reptile brain, which supposedly
controls eating, sex, and ritual, and then on top of that formed
the limbic or mammal brain, which controls emotion, and
finally on top of that the neo-cortex, huge in comparison,
which accounts for abstract thought and differentiates us from
other creatures, which perhaps isn't considered to be quite
true any longer. Aren't they figuring out that in some small
way apes can actually abstract? At any rate, thus the attraction
we often have for certain animals and the vague sense of
recognition or affinity we may feel. It's interesting to think
that the attraction Lawrence feels for his snake at the water
trough may not only have a mythological basis—he calls
him a "king in exile, uncrowned in the underworld"—but a
physiological one a well. Jung talks about the serpent in our
abdomen. True, and we also have one in our brain. Seeing
the snake jars some kinship in the R-complex, the reptile
brain. The same thing happens to the persona in my poem
"The Copperhead." He becomes fascinated by this snake
sitting out on a tree limb that's fallen into a pond. He just
wants to get closer and closer because something in him is

drawing him to it. Just as in the Lawrence poem the tension arises between his fear, a product of his "human education," as he says, and a deeply felt affinity.

Suarez: So this is where those animal poems in *Shooting Rats* came from?

Bottoms: Yes, the poems in the section called "All the Animal Inside Us"—"Crawling Out at Parties," "The Copperhead," "Watching Gators at Ray Boone's Reptile Farm," and the rest. But the reptile brain is still essential to me, literally a part of me. And everyone else. Occasionally it still creeps out of the shadows when it recognizes a distant relative in the real world—most recently, perhaps, in the poem "In a Kitchen, Late," which is in the new section of *Armored Hearts*. The conduit into the wilderness there is a cockroach. The persona is sitting at the kitchen table snacking on chicken, and he feels a roach in the hairs of his leg. Disgusting, true. But it becomes for him an odd connection to the darkness and the woods outside, to something he feels he's lost.

Suarez: What creatures serve as the most effective conduits for you?

Bottoms: Snakes, turtles, alligators, rats, vultures. I tend not to be as fascinated by the nobler animals, say Warren's eagles or even James Wright's horses, but I tend to run with the lower order. Neruda says, "It has never occurred to me to speak/ with the genteel animals." He wanted to speak with the serpents. I feel the same way. That same sensibility is developed much further in Theodore Roethke, and this must have been where I first encountered it. He loved what he called the "minimal," the elemental, and in his greenhouse poems he even extends it into the plant world. But he has his animals too—slugs, mice, lizards, fish. His little poem "The Meadow Mouse" has always been one of my favorites. He calls it "My thumb of a child that nuzzled in my palm."

Suarez: Do you see any connection between Roethke's meadow mouse and your rats of "Shooting Rats at the Bibb County Dump"?

Bottoms: Indirectly, yes. That aspect of Roethke probably made a poem like "Shooting Rats" possible. But my approach in "Shooting Rats" is not typical of the animal poems we've been taking about, which take an approach similar to Roethke, an approach through affinity, or in the case of "The Meadow Mouse" we might even say affection. This stance is a little more enlightened than the persona of "Shooting Rats," who doesn't see anything particularly cuddly about these rats at the garbage dump and feels only a vague and perverse similarity of fate. Nevertheless, Dickey told me once that I'd created about as much sympathy for a rat as anyone could hope to create. But this is reader sympathy, at the persona's expense. Roethke's attitude toward his meadow mouse is a recognition of kinship. In that recognition lie his connections with the spiritual undercurrents.

Suarez: You see poetry as a means of re-accessing the primal.

Bottoms: Certainly, but not only the primal world, the primal self, in the sense that poetry is self-exploration, a journey into the darker and more dangerous coves of one's own psyche.

Suarez: What do you mean by dangerous here?

Bottoms: Well, poetry can be dangerous in the sense that the poet often has to confront things about himself or herself—fears, impulses, desires, repressed memories—that may not be exactly pleasant. In fact, they may be ugly, troubling, and even very frightening. Let me explain that with a metaphor. Fishing provides a good one for writing this kind of poem. You're out there alone in some cove in the little poetry boat, throwing out your lure—a good word here—and you're casting down into the depths, the psychic depths. Of course, you're going for the creative impulse, the stuff of the great poem, in our metaphor you're going for the seven-pound bass, but you don't know what's down there. You just have to be willing to cast out that Jitterbug or that Mirr-O-Lure or that Rooster Tail and take whatever hits the line. I see all of this again in relation to an idea Jung had about creativity, that the seeds of creativity are mixed into what he calls "slime from the depth," that psychic slime where the ugliest and most animalistic aspects of our personalities reside. These are all those fearful things we've confined, repressed into our subconscious. But if you're after the creative impulse, you have to be willing to wallow around in that. Or coming back to our metaphor, you have to be willing to drag up whatever hits your lure—gar, copperhead, water moccasin, alligator. When we confront the lower beasts of our psyche, we can be in for a dangerous encounter.

Suarez: Your themes don't seem to have changed much over the course of your career. If anything the poems may have gotten somewhat darker. I know that you are happily married now and have a beautiful five-year-old daughter. How do you account for that bleakness of vision?

Bottoms: My friend Dave Smith wrote in an essay somewhere that all poems are about two things—life and death. I wrote a little piece a few years later and said that he was at least half right—all poems are really about death. We talk about this is a lot in my classes, and one thing I like to point out to students is a book that turns up in Woody Allen's movie *Annie Hall*. Woody Allen and Diane Keeton are working on a relationship, a problem since he's the typical neurotic New Yorker and she's so sunny she wears flowers on her hat. Well, they walk into this bookstore. He's just met her and wants to impress her, cue her in on everything that's important to him and such, so he takes her over to the psychology section. He reaches up and pulls a book off the shelf and the camera zooms in. It's Ernest Becker's *The Denial of Death*. Of course, its a pretty funny moment, but the first time I saw the movie, I was startled by that because I'd just finished reading *The Denial of Death*. A great book. Becker's premise is that the only real truth in our lives is our death. It's our one undeniable fact, nothing we can do about it, and Becker says that all the other aspects of our personalities are geared to deny it. They're all lies. Of course, they're very healthy and necessary lies. Otherwise we'd just step out in front of some truck. One of the best metaphors Becker uses to illustrate the nature of the personality is an onion. This onion represents the whole of your personality. You take it, put it down on the table, and slice it in half. The core is your death—the fact at the center—and all the layers built up around it are the various layers of your personality, all of your interests, your ambitions, the things you involve yourself in—I'm going to be a great poet, I'm going to be a great pianist, I'm going to be a great painter—the stuff that makes you believe in a future. Well, these things are only distractions, denials, lies. As life-affirming as they may be, they won't save us from our one undeniable fact. Where are Whitman and Emily Dickinson? Where's Vladimir Horowitz? Where are Gauguin, Matisse, Picasso? But here's the point. These things, even though they are lies, are the material out of which we create art. This is the stuff from which we make poems and stories. So, in that sense, all poems are about death. At the heart, at the core, there's always that fundamental truth. Even the sunniest poem has this kind of death shadow, this dark spot at the core.

Suarez: In a recent review, Benjamin Griffith points out that many of the new poems in *Armored Hearts* are more openly Christian in their themes than your previous work. Could you comment on that?

Bottoms: Yes, I suppose he's right about that. I've been concerned over the last few years, maybe since the birth of my daughter, with the possibility of living a Christian life in our culture. So much in American life, at least in the popular culture, seems to mitigate against it. Perhaps this was always the case, but at forty-seven I seem to be getting more perspective on it. No, I don't actually believe that. I don't believe it was always the case. Things that were once relegated to the underworld are now mainstream virtues of pop culture. We've generally lost our ethical foundations. You don't have to look farther than the local movie theater or music store to see what virtues our culture holds in high esteem—violence, murder, rape, drugs, promiscuity, the general abuse of women. Of course, this view is very simplistic because I'm speaking so generally. Ours is a complex culture. Not everyone in America holds those values. But a significant number of people have developed a frightening tolerance of them, more than is healthy, and they generally have the advantage of fashion and fad. To make the situation even more perverse, among some folks— including many academics—traditional values are now thought to be deviant. The problem of the Christian in our culture no longer seems to be the task of converting the masses, which has become overwhelming, but the problem of survival without withdrawing entirely from the world.

Suarez: How do these things relate to poetry today?

Bottoms: Well, poetry is individual vision. Pure art has no moral responsibility or agenda. But generally speaking, poetry seems to me an antidote of sorts against much of our trouble—at least to the extent that it seeks to put us all in touch with our common humanity. Jung believed that in our rush to technology, Western societies lost touch with myth, and thus we lost our souls. I like to think of poetry, and all art, as the act of getting back in touch with the soul. The great difficulty in America is getting people to listen. Most folks are numb to the spiritual possibilities in their lives. As

Ed Hirsch says in his poem "For the Sleepwalkers," "We have to drink the stupefying cup of darkness/ and wake up to ourselves, nourished and surprised." This is no easy task, but there are a significant number of people in this country who have not been totally dulled by television and Hollywood. Here's an interesting irony. Over the last few years, what has probably generated the most public interest in poetry is not a poem or a book of poems, but a film. I'm speaking of *Il Postino*, the film about Pablo Neruda exiled on a Greek island. It's marvelous to see how this semi-literate postman's encounter with Neruda opens up his life to the possibility of beauty and meaning. I'll bet Neruda's book sales have gone through the roof because of that movie. I hope so. I'd like to think that this could be the first step for many people who are thoughtful but still strangers to poetry. You'll note, though, that it's a foreign film. It was not made in Hollywood. American pop culture generally refuses to make its audience think, to confront meaningful issues such as values and faith. Oh, occasionally you'll see a TV sitcom deal with some current social issue—gay rights or interracial relationships, the juicer the better—but how many prime time programs have ever dealt with the problems religious faith? Or have even suggested that anyone should think twice about such? Unfortunately, not many of our so-called "serious writers" even seem willing to deal with these questions, as though they were conveniently no longer relevant. The Greek poet C.P. Cavafy has a wonderful little poem called "The First Step" where he calls all poets "citizens of the city of ideas." I like that. But we need to remember also that there is good citizenship and bad citizenship. To be a good citizen of "the city of ideas" a writer must act in a responsible manner. This requires honesty of sentiment and approach. It also requires that a writer not trivialize, not turn his or her face from the important questions.

Suarez: Let's use that to dig back into your own poetry. I remember in an early poem called "The Boy Shepherds' Simile" you talk about a time when "believing was an easy thing." Can you say something about the origins of that poem and what it tries to accomplish?

Bottoms: I was raised in Canton, Georgia, a small town about fifty miles north of Atlanta, and got my religious education at the Canton First Baptist Church. In the late 50s—when I was six, seven, and eight—my mother was superintendent of the Primary Department of the Sunday School. Every year, of course, they'd have the annual Christmas pageant—a manger scene on the front lawn—and when she couldn't recruit enough boys to play the parts of Joseph and the shepherds, which was always a problem, she didn't hesitate to draft me into service. For a boy that age, this meant a large dose of embarrassment—the indignity of being dressed in an old sheet, of having to hold a crooked stick and stand out in the cold beside a cow or goat, whatever animal could be dredged up off a farm, and also the horror of having all my friends come around with their Polaroids to take pictures that might be passed out at school. Children can find terror in the most innocent things. Anyway, the poem is spoken by one of these boy shepherds who is grown now and remembering those scenes. He's simply asking why anyone would go through that. He says, "This was not a child or a king,/ but Mary Sosebee's Christmas doll of a year ago." Just a doll. So what does this have to do with adoration and devotion? What does it have to do with worship? The answer comes then in the simile "But it was like a king." Whether or not the simile has any meaning depends, I suppose, on faith.

Suarez: But you imply a contrast between the relative ease of a child's faith as opposed to the more difficult faith of an adult. For the culture as a whole, is faith a more difficult question in the 90s than it was in the 50s?

Bottoms: Probably. These times are less childlike, more cynical, more permissive. But faith has always been difficult. Most everything in the world argues against it. Just take history. How could God have permitted the holocaust? Or the suffering of the early Christians at the hands of the Romans? Or the slaughter of the Jews during the Roman occupation of Jerusalem? According to Josephus, during the First Roman-Jewish war, over three thousand Jews were crucified in one day. Our times, at least in this country, are not so generally bloody. But yes, faith is a difficult matter, and coming to terms with human violence is far from the only threat. Our current myth is science, and science denies completely the ability to know except through the methods of science. We don't often talk about tension or conflict in poetry, at least not to the degree we discuss it in fiction, but conflict is important for creating intrigue in all art. What interests me very much are the poetic possibilities in the tension between the spiritual and the secular, what happens when these two realms collide, and the survival strategies faith seeks to employ. I tried to get at some of that in several of the new poems in *Armored Hearts*.

Suarez: Is "The Blue Mountains" an example of that collision?

Bottoms: Yes. That poem comes from a story about my wife's family. She's from western Montana and was raised in fairly strict fundamentalist church. The poem is about her niece and her niece's husband who also belonged to a fundamentalist denomination. Anyway, one night a deacon in their church had a dream that God was going to burn Portland because of its sinful doings. This was supposed to happen at a certain time, and so when the date got close this woman and her husband gathered their two-year-old, packed whatever they could into a van, and literally headed for the hills. Of course, Portland didn't burn. God apparently spared it. Well, when I heard about this, I couldn't believe it. How stupid, I thought, for these two kids—they were both very young—to leave their home and jobs and cart their baby off to the mountains. All to flee a nightmare sparked by someone's bad Mexican dinner. But then as I started to write the poem, as I started to involve myself in the situation, I had a change of heart. The more I got into the thing, the more I liked them. Eventually, I started thinking, "Now, that's real faith. I wish I had a faith like that." I came to see it as a faith one could put to some literal use in the world. The poem ends though on a note of ambiguity, and I wanted that. In the last few lines they seem reluctant to talk about what appears to have been their folly, but they've discovered something too. What they like to talk about instead are the owls they heard in the mountains during the boat trips they took. What they've experienced, of course, can be read as metaphor. The owls in the distance are heralding out those narrow passes.

Suarez: Griffith writes in his essay that your attention to "emptiness" reminds him of a concept Flannery O'Connor was attracted to in the work of Pierre Teilhard de Chardin, namely "passive diminishment," or as Griffith says, "the serene acceptance of inevitable loss." Would you comment on this in relation to the later poems?

Bottoms: I believe he was talking about that poem "Allatoona Evening," which I put at the end of the book. But what he says generally holds true for my later poems. I think what many are trying to do, especially in the last half of *Armored Hearts*, is find a gradual sort of working toward resignation and peace. Elizabeth Bishop says, "The art of losing isn't hard to master," but we all feel the tragic irony there. Christianity provides some help, of course, through a shedding of false ambition, which only creates in us anger and frustration. Poetry helps here also. That's what "Allatoona Evening" is about. It's an important poem for me in many ways, a poem that came out of many frustrations—about writing and teaching and other things—and I think the key lines of the poem are the ones that equate anger and ambition. The persona is out beside this lake at evening—he's going fishing—and it's a very peaceful scene, and suddenly he senses that the whippoorwills and the bats are telling him to lay down all his anger. "Lay it down, they say, your ambition,/ which is only anger,/ which sated could bring you to no better place." That's a powerfully healing thought for me. Even if all our ambitions, which are generally misplaced anyway, were realized, they could bring us to no better spiritual place than this one moment beside this lake with "these three stars soaking up twilight." I like the ending of that poem as much as any I've ever written.

Suarez: You said poetry helps us achieve this resignation. How does it help?

Bottoms: Well, in a number of ways. For one, it helps us ask the right questions about our lives. Literature never solves any of the great problems, of course, but it does help us define the significant questions, and in this way provides a focus that helps us avoid the temptations of the superficial. I don't think that can be said about American culture in general, pop art I mean. I'll give you one other way poetry can help too. Our whole lives are extended exercises in learning to accept loss. But as I've said before, literature can achieve a curious emotional bargain with death. Not that death negotiates very much. Still, a deal can be struck, good things may be wrenched from despair. Out of a good poem we can get understanding, resignation, empathy, even beauty. Occasionally in really fine poetry we may even find an aesthetic or emotional affirmation and transcendence.

Suarez: What do you mean by that? Could you give us an example?

Bottoms: Sure. I love a little poem by Warren called "After the Dinner Party." The narrative runs something like this. An old couple is sitting around their table late at night. The dinner party is over, the guests are gone, the fire is burning down in the fireplace. Everything about the scene suggests an ending of things. They talk of the past for while, of their children who are away and building their own lives. It's painfully clear that they understand the past is gone and that they can expect no real future. The woman snuffs out the candles and they sit quietly in the last light of the fire. Then Warren writes: "Soon the old stairs/ Will creak to a briefness of light, then true weight of darkness, and then/ That heart-dimness in which neither joy nor sorrow counts." Now what could be darker than that? What could be bleaker and more honest? No joy in the past or the future, no sorrow, no human emotion will stop their inevitable separation. Then the last line, "Even so, one hand gropes out for another, again." An amazing affirmation—not of the past or the future, but of the only thing left, the moment. This is what real poetry can do, even against the inevitability of death. It can take the terrible, the frightening, the tragic, and transform it into something positive, something we might even call beautiful. Yes, I think that is a powerful help.

A BAKED TORTILLA SCORCHED
WITH THE FACE OF CHRIST
An Interview Conducted by William Walsh

This interview developed from several talks held at Georgia State University over the course of the summer of 2005, shortly after the publication of Bottoms' *Waltzing through the Endtime*. It was done for the Tenth Anniversary issue of *Five Points: A Journal of Literature and Art*.

Walsh: Before we talk about poetry let's talk about *Five Points* for a moment. This issue marks the tenth anniversary of the magazine. In a culture where literary magazines crop up and die almost immediately that's a big deal. What's the secret here?

Bottoms: Friends, I think. Wonderful writers who were generous from the first. And also the people who've worked with the magazine. When Pam Durban and I started—Pam was co-editor then—we made a list of folks we really wanted to publish, and we just made a few phone calls and wrote some letters. The response we received was remarkable. Pam is a fine fiction writer and a good person, well respected, so she had a strong network of fiction people to draw from. And I knew a good number of folks too. Dave Smith and I had edited an anthology back in the mid-eighties, *The Morrow Anthology of Younger American Poets*, which had included just over a hundred of the best American poets born after 1940. For a great many of those folks that was their first anthology appearance, so when I asked some of them to contribute to *Five Points*, they responded in a very generous way.

Walsh: So the magazine was started by you and Pam Durban?

Bottoms: No, not really. *Five Points* was the idea of Bob Sattelmeyer, who was chair of the English Department at the time. Bob came to us and asked if we were interested in starting a magazine. Of course, we were, under the condition that we had sufficient resources. Years earlier I'd kicked around the idea of a magazine, but couldn't find any money anywhere. Anyway, Bob had the vision and the wherewithal to make it happen. He found a small hunk of money, and we got things rolling. And he faithfully kept us going. Without Bob, there would be no *Five Points*.

Over the years, too, we've received strong support from the administration, and we've found good friends in the community, business folks such as Bud Blanton, who chairs our advisory board, and Mike Easterly, who's sort of a patron saint. Our greatest blessing, though, has been Megan Sexton. She's the real heart of the magazine. More than any other person, she's responsible for whatever success we've had. She's a fine writer herself and an enormously talented editor.

She runs the magazine at every level and does a terrific job. Without her we'd likely just close up shop.

Walsh: You've never stated any specific editorial policy, and the magazine seems to have been always somewhat eclectic. But what do you look for in poem or a story?

Bottoms: Yes, we've tried to be open to different approaches, open to material that works on its own terms. That's the only healthy way to run a magazine, of course. Otherwise you simply become a mouthpiece for some literary fad or theory. Basically we look for excellence and control, for imaginative pieces that demonstrate concern for an audience. And, of course, we look for that vague but essential thing we call art, which each poem or story, if it works well, will define for itself in some unique way. I might say also that I don't care much for wit for its own sake.

Walsh: Poems and stories can't be humorous?

Bottoms: Well, there's a place for humor, of course. But humor itself is never the goal. Wit should always serve some deeper purpose. There's a little poem ["Metier"] by Jack Gilbert that I like. It goes like this: "The Greek fishermen do not / play on the beach and I don't / write funny poems." I like that a lot. The Greek fishermen are in the business of dredging up something from the depths. That's serious business. Poets and writers, I think, are in the same business. So I watch for those pieces that try to reach something deeper, try to ask the hard questions, look for some universal significance in the particulars they deal with. I think this is what all serious art is about—that exploration, that seeking, which is not only an external search, but an inward search as well.

Walsh: You speak of this as though it were a kind of spiritual awakening.

Bottoms: It's not dissimilar, I think. A religious service may be the only place some folks have experienced that sort of emotional intensity. A few others may have found it in a particularly moving piece of music, or say a painting. But many people, I think, have never experienced it at all. You certainly won't find in popular culture many keys to unlock the inner life.

Walsh: Story is very important to you, and you're often called a narrative poet. But in your classes you constantly emphasize the importance of metaphor, the importance of the figurative in poetry. And often your own poems have a very hard figurative turn. How do you view the use of metaphor? And is it consciously there in the beginning of the poem or does it derive from the poem as you work on it?

Bottoms: Many of the earlier poems, the shorter poems, do have a big figurative leap. And in those cases the figurative device was usually the seed of the poem. About narrative and metaphor, well, they're certainly not at odds with each other. Metaphor, though, is the main ingredient in the recipe. It's the way the poem suggests connections to the larger world, the way the poem reaches beyond itself for the seen and unseen world. My poems tell stories, sure, but good poems want to tap something below the narrative surface. They want to mine the universal, and one way they do this is by discovering the metaphorical possibilities in our everyday lives—which causes us to see things in a different way, of course, to see an expanded world, a world with new dimensions.

Walsh: Can you think of an example where the figurative device, as you say, was the seed of the poem?

Bottoms: Oh sure. Take that poem about the vulture tree. The notion of the vultures as "dwarfed transfiguring angels" was actually the seed of that poem, and the last line—"with mercy enough to consume us all and give us wings"—was the first line that came to me. In those early poems, say the first four books or so, that was the way it usually happened for me. I could probably name a dozen or so poems where the last line contains the figurative device and was actually the first line to be written. But the figurative can certainly find unexpected ways of rising out of the writing process. This is what we hope for, right?

Walsh: What about the longer poems? Do they come in a similar way?

Bottoms: I don't know. Maybe. But it's hard to make generalizations. I'm thinking now of that poem "Easter Shoes Epistle," and the metaphor of faith being something like an old shoe. That's where that poem started. Still, many of the longer ones don't rely on a central controlling metaphor, so it's hard to make that generalization.

Walsh: "Homage to Buck Cline," which is the centerpiece of that book [*Waltzing through the Endtime*], may be one of those. Still, it has that strong religious metaphor at the end. I mean, you make him a saint, but the metaphor is something that you build toward. The poem is about you getting stopped for speeding when you were a teenager, and it develops that narrative, but it's also pulls in much more.

Bottoms: It tries to, anyway. It's one of the first of those longer narratives I've been writing, those sort of fractured narratives that jump around a good bit.

Walsh: What do you mean by "fractured"?

Bottoms: Well, stories that sort of break up at various places and take a thoughtful breath. Or related stories that are woven into each other, or patched together with little scraps of meditation. It's just a narrative technique—a piece of a story, a flashback, a sidestep, another piece of the story.

Walsh: So basically this form gives you a chance to think about and comment somewhat on the stories you tell.

Bottoms: Sure, that's a large part of it.

Walsh: "Homage to Buck Cline" sounds very autobiographical. How much of it actually is?

Bottoms: Oh, most all of it. I don't think there's even one invented detail. Buck was the chief of police in Canton, Georgia, when I grew up there in the sixties. And he was literally 6'5" or so, and must have weighed around 280. He had a reputation for being about as sour and generally mean as a human being gets. Whether that was true or not, I don't know, but that was his reputation. And he'd made that reputation by keeping the young toughs in the county in line. Everybody in our high school feared Buck Cline like the devil himself, even the guys who considered themselves tough, which of course, I did not.

Walsh: Especially that night.

Bottoms: True. The poem focuses on a night just after I'd turned sixteen and got my driver's license. Anyway, I had a steady girlfriend, who was fifteen or sixteen, and her mother was teaching her to cook. Back then the stomach was still thought to be the way to a man's heart.

At least, in Canton, Georgia. So my girlfriend liked to make these spaghetti suppers for us, and her mother encouraged her by supplying candles and a bottle of Mateus Rosé, which she had to drive down to the county line to buy. That was very adult, you know. And, of course, we thought it was very romantic. Anyway, one Saturday night around 12:30 or 1:00 in the morning, after a couple of glasses of Mateus, I was driving home and was stopped at the traffic light on the edge of town. Across the street, about fifty yards to my right, I saw Buck Cline parked in his patrol car in the shadows of the North Canton Store. Buck was keeping an eye on the would-be hoods circling our one burger joint. Well, I was feeling a little too full of myself, on the Mateus, I guess, and I got the strange notion that if I eased through the light and put about fifty yards between Buck Cline and my car, I could floor it, spin some rubber for the guys at the burger joint, and out-run Buck to my house, which was only about three miles away. "The imp of the perverse," Poe calls it, and pretty stupid. The poem centers on what happened when Buck pulled me over about a mile and half down the highway, took my license, and found out my name. I'm not the real David Bottoms, my dad is—I'm only the junior version. Well, my dad was a veteran, a sailor who was severely wounded at the naval battle of Guadalcanal—he served on the USS *Atlanta*. And like most men of that generation, Buck Cline was a veteran also. Canton was a small town, but I had no idea they knew each other. What I discovered was the secret bond that existed between those guys, those veterans. And also, I suppose, I discovered for the first time—at least firsthand—that there are relationships in the world that were formed way before our time, relationships that affect us in profound ways.

Walsh: Things we used to attribute to the stars, you say in the poem. By which, I take you to mean fate and all that.

Bottoms: That's right. Buck Cline's respect for my father saved me from a trip to the county jail. That certainly opened up my world view. Suddenly the world was not just me and my immediate relationship to it, but there was a world before me, a network of events and relationships that developed before me, relationships on which every aspect of my life depended. And not only that, this network of events and relationships would continue to go on after me, and certainly be influenced, at least to some very small degree, by my own life.

Walsh: You call him "Saint Buck" at the end of the poem. Quite a shift in opinion.

Bottoms: "Saint Buck /of the handy blackjack." He was, I suppose, at that particular moment, a pretty unlikely vehicle for grace. But Saint Buck still sounds about right. The moment had that sort of intensity for me, I guess. And, of course, it scared the crap out of me.

Walsh: As you say, though, the poem is not just about Buck Cline, but about your father, about memory, about the way the past intersects our lives. I wonder if you could've written a poem like this twenty or even ten years ago. Obviously, you've carried this memory around since you were sixteen, but only recently found the right vehicle for it.

Bottoms: I could've written a poem about Buck Cline, sure. But it wouldn't have been anything like that poem. Twenty years ago I would have brought a very different sensibility to the subject. The poem would've been a more focused, more straight-forward narrative. I thought a long time about this poem, about the Buck Cline incident I mean. Oh, a good number of years ago I knew it was something I wanted to write about, but I wasn't sure just how to approach it. You remember what Hemingway said in "The Snows of Kilimanjaro" about saving certain things to write about until he knew enough to write them. I don't know if putting off the Buck Cline poem was that conscious a thing, but there may have been something of that. I needed to discover a more open form. Some of that I picked up from Robert Penn Warren, I think, some from Charles Wright, and some from other folks, of course.

Walsh: I'll bet you were thinking of Warren's "Audubon."

Bottoms: Of course. I love what Warren was able to do there. He puzzled over that poem for years, I think, trying to figure out a way to capture Audubon's story. Then one morning it just sort of came to him. I think he said he was making up his bed, and for some unknown reason, the notion of snapshots of Audubon's life occurred to him. Rather than a straightforward narrative, he'd do snaps that would capture critical events and characteristics, and also give rise to association, meditation, and such. It was a wonderful breakthrough for Warren, and it gave us a magnificent poem. A few early Dave Smith poems work that way also, and most all of Charles Wright's later poetry, though Charles depends far less on narrative. Anyway, the form or method, or whatever you want to call it, appeals a great deal to me now. It's a new kind of freedom. It allows the poem to develop much more on association.

Walsh: And often the association is metaphorical.

Bottoms: Sure.

Walsh: One metaphor that runs through your work at every stage is water and the afterlife. I think you said somewhere that your first encounter with figurative language came from church.

Bottoms: Yes, I believe I said Sunday school at the First Baptist Church in Canton, Georgia. When I was a boy my mother was superintendent of the Primary Department, and so I spent a good deal of time there. Those old hymns, I suppose, were the first place I ran across language being used in a figurative way. "Shall we gather at the river," that's still one of my favorites. Or a song like "The Old Gospel Ship," which the Carter family did. "I'm gonna take a trip on that old gospel ship." And, of course, in scripture. Mostly, the psalms, I suppose. But there's so much water imagery in those hymns. It's the whole beautiful notion of crossing over, of getting to the other side. This imagery, of course, is ancient, and not uniquely Christian, but I suppose Sunday school largely accounts for my love of it. Also, as you know, lakes and rivers make such wonderful metaphors for the psyche—the conscious mind and the unconscious, the surface and those hidden depths below the surface. I keep coming back to that, I guess.

Walsh: You talk a good deal about Carl Jung in your poetry workshops. About Jung's idea of the collective unconscious.

Bottoms: That's right. I don't understand half of what I read by Jung, but what I do catch continues to fascinate me. I love the notion of the unconscious as the repository of the archetype, and I like to try to apply that to the creative process. I find that it's a good way to talk to students about the act of poetry, to turn them inward, to get them thinking about their own creative process and the mysteries that process connects them to.

Walsh: This turns up in a poem from your *Waltzing* book. I'm thinking of "Melville in the Bass Boat." The persona is sort of fishing for ideas, right?

Bottoms: In a way, sure. I think the poem wants to say something about the creative process, about the unconscious and the way the idea hits. The persona is out on a deep lake, fishing, at night. He's trying to "conjure one small mystery caged in the bones of a fish." But nothing is happening. Oddly enough, as if he'd anticipated his luck, he's brought along some reading, of all things a copy of *Moby Dick*. He begins to read by lantern light and his mind drifts into Melville's story, the *Pequod*, Melville's descriptions of the sea. Then the persona's present moment and Melville's narrative start to merge a little, and suddenly the "dream-fish" strikes "far out, like a thought." The poem plays on a line from Melville— "... Meditation and water are wedded for ever." I love that line. It catches perfectly the way nature bends us toward pondering the big mysteries.

Walsh: Fishing has always been important to you. And animals associated with water.

Bottoms: Yes, I used to fish a lot, especially when I lived in Florida. But I haven't been fishing in years. I stopped when my daughter was young—she thought it was boring—and I never got back to it. But I've always been very attracted to it, the sense of mystery, you know. The sense of dredging something up out of the depths. And as you say, to the turtles, snakes, rats, and other creatures that you find around lakes and rivers. Someone told once me that Warren and Dickey took all the noble animals—the eagles, the owls, the horses, and such—and I got stuck with the creatures of a somewhat lower order. It's true, I suppose. But they tell a story too, don't they? The reptiles, I mean. And the amphibians.

They're wallowers in the muck and slime. Roethke loved them, and he was always one of my favorites. The wigglers and slimy ones. They gave him some fine poems. "Slug" comes immediately to mind, and "The Lizard." And, of course, all of that greenhouse slime—the tendrils, the scum, the leaf-mold. All of these things speak of beginnings and transformations, and I'm very interested in that.

Walsh: And in your new book, I think, you're also interested in endings. Endings and perhaps transformations. And the animals are still there playing a role—the snakes and rats anyway.

Bottoms: The end time, you mean.

Walsh: I think a very interesting development has taken place in your work. It started in *Vagrant Grace*, but has matured in *Waltzing through the Endtime*. There's a shift, a spiritual transcendence, away from the world of the earlier poems. The animals of the world are still there to some degree in the new book, yet the metaphor is more spiritual, and the focus is more apocalyptic. I mean, if a person didn't know the new book was written by you, he'd most likely not guess. That is, outside of a few titles such as "Shooting Rats in the Afterlife."

Bottoms: The new book is much more of what I've always wanted my poems to be. I'm interested in what you said about this spiritual shift. I don't really think the poems have shifted so much toward the spiritual—I think I've always worked toward that, at trying to be what Warren calls a "seeker." But there is a significant shift toward a Christian outlook. A very liberal one for sure, but still it's a spiritual quest that frames itself in Christian mythology. Anyway, this is all to say that *Waltzing through the Endtime* is a quirky sort of book. It's apocalyptic in many ways, and it deals with wacky speculations about the afterlife and the problems of living a spiritual life in a secular and scientific age. And, as we've said, the poems have also evolved stylistically. They've stretched their muscles a little. The stories are still there and they remain central, but the poems pause to think about them more, and to think not only about their consequences for our everyday lives but to think about their ultimate consequences.

Walsh: For instance, what does it mean that in 1977 a woman in Phoenix, Arizona, baked a tortilla scorched with the face of Christ? That's from "Vigilance," right? And there are several other very weird appearances in there. I'm wondering where that poem came from.

Bottoms: A number of things, I guess. My fascination for wacky appearances of the Deity, of course, but also a dream my mother-in-law had. Mostly, though, the seed of the whole thing was a talk I had with Barry Hannah, the Mississippi novelist. A few years ago I saw Barry at the Sewanee Writer's Conference. He'd just finished a bout of chemotherapy and was getting strong again, and he told me that when he was in intensive care in Oxford, Mississippi, Jesus had appeared to him. He looked up, he said, and Jesus was standing at the foot of his bed, a big man with a barrel chest. Barry was very sincere, and I was moved by that. He looked at Jesus and said, "I've neglected you." And Jesus said nothing, or smiled. I can't really remember. But it was a moving story, and it brought up a memory of my father-in-law, how one night in a deserted part of northwest Montana he'd seen Christ standing on the shoulder of the road. True story. He was a serious fundamentalist, and he ran a paper route way out in the boonies of Montana. He'd drive a couple of hundred miles on this route, very late at night, and he'd listen to gospel music on the tape deck in his truck. Suddenly one night, Jesus was standing on the side of the road. Anyway, I wove these stories together with several others, including a dream my mother-in-law had about floating down a river on an outhouse—true—which I parallel with a little line of scripture about the second coming: "If the good man of the house had known when the thief would come."

Walsh: Your mother-in-law dreamed about floating down a river on an outhouse?

Bottoms: You'd have to know her.

Walsh: Let's go back to this notion of the poet as "seeker." You talked about that recently in an essay. That phrase is from Warren?

Bottoms: Actually, he may have used the word "yearner." But the words are synonymous. He mentioned that in an interview he did with *The Gettysburg Review* editor Peter Stitt, back in the seventies, I think. He said he was a yearner after meaning. He didn't have any particular theology to assign to the world, but he was a yearner for meaning. He sensed, I think, some sort of intrinsic meaning in the world, something he couldn't quite put his finger on, but it was enough of a hint to make him yearn for more. I like that very much, and I think that all serious writers are yearners. They're seekers after the big answers, what Warren called in his poem "I'm Dreaming of a White Christmas" the logic of "the original dream." We'll never know those big answers, of course, because we're only a part of the dream, not the dreamer, but the serious writer yearns nevertheless. And what the writer yearns for, what he or she seeks, is a sense of consequence in the world.

Walsh: The writer has an inherent need for meaning?

Bottoms: I don't know about that. But this is something, I think, that comes from the world itself. The world is constantly teasing us about this, constantly dropping little clues to the mystery. But the world is very coy, I think. It doesn't want to give us the whole story, not in one piece anyway. I remember Dickey telling me once that he occasionally experienced these little epiphanies, these moments of clarity in his life, when he felt that if he could just connect them all together, like you might connect the dots, he'd have a perfect blueprint of reality. The key here, I think, is the word "felt." We feel sometimes that we might actually break through the fog of the world into some ultimate clarity, yet we're pretty limited, aren't we? Nevertheless, we yearn for that breakthrough. You remember what Tolstoy said on his death bed? "Search, always go on searching."

Walsh: Your work has often been compared to Dickey's. What was your relationship with him like?

Bottoms: We were friends. We always got along well. He liked to assume the role of a father figure with young writers he liked. He'd say, "You're one of mine" and such stuff. But we were friends for about sixteen years, I guess. I've always heard stories about Dickey's outrageous behavior. You know the stories, Dickey got drunk and insulted so-and-so, or made a pass at a professor's wife. Or pulled off some equally obnoxious stunt. If you don't know them, you can find just about every one in Henry Hart's biography. But, truthfully, he never behaved badly in front of me. He stayed at our house several times back in the eighties. The first time he came, his wife, Debba, phoned me to ask that I not take him to a liquor store. On the way home from the airport Jim asked me if she'd called. What could I say? And how could I tell James Dickey I wasn't going to take him to a liquor store. He sort of sensed that I was in a bad spot though, so he suggested that we make a pact. I'd stop at a liquor store, but we'd only buy beer. That was the way we played it. When he came to my house he'd only drink beer, actually I think it was Country Club malt liquor. We had a good relationship, though I didn't see him much during the last few years. I'd talk to him on the phone occasionally, and I talked with him a few days before he died.

Walsh: Did you ever read one another's work in the early stages? Would he hand you an early version of a poem?

Bottoms: Oh no, he'd never do that. He wouldn't have been able to give up that sort of authority. Actually, we hardly ever talked about each other's poetry. We probably talked more about sports or music. I'd played guitar in several little bluegrass and country bands. He was very interested in that sort of thing.

Walsh: He was a guitar player, right?

Bottoms: He loved folk music. Southern folk music, I mean, traditional mountain music and bluegrass. He loved guitars and owned a bunch of them, but he wasn't really much of a guitar player. Ironically, he didn't have a very good sense of rhythm. He did know a good deal about the music though, especially the guitar players. He loved Doc Watson and Merle Travis and worked hard to get that finger-picking style.

Walsh: How do you think traditional music influenced his writing? And yours?

Bottoms: Oh, I don't know. I'd have to really think about that. Dickey's writing anyway. But I'm sure it was a very large influence. Two or three poems come to mind. "Buckdancer's Choice" is my favorite. I think Dickey uses it there in a pretty conventional way, a voice that has to express itself even in the most depressing conditions, but it's a wonderful poem. It takes its title from an old guitar piece that was recorded by Sam McGee.

Walsh: You read that poem at his memorial service at the University of South Carolina. Did you choose that one for any particular reason?

Bottoms: Well, it's a fine poem. Always one of my favorites, and for the life-affirming spirit it communicates. It's about

Dickey's mother, you know. And how, even though she has "breathless angina," she still finds the strength to whistle that old tune. She still finds the strength to whistle up a little joy.

Walsh: And in your own poems, has music been a large influence?

Bottoms: Sure. Music is a large part of my life. But influences are hard to pinpoint. I mean people are always trying to draw parallels between music and poetry, and I think they're very indistinct. Any influence on my own work probably comes from the imagery of those old traditional songs, and the gospel songs most especially.

Walsh: We're back to the church music again.

Bottoms: To some degree, sure. But I'm also talking about those old mountain ballads too, and those murdered lover songs and hobo songs and work songs. But yes, gospel music has been very important.

Walsh: I'm very interested in poetic influences and how they sort of create a lineage of poetic history. You're often associated with Warren and Dickey, with the narrative line in Southern poetry, but who do you see as your most crucial influences?

Bottoms: That's hard to say. I came late to Warren and Dickey. When I started writing poetry as an undergrad at Mercer—that would have been in the late sixties and early seventies—I was very taken with Dylan Thomas. Everybody was then, it seemed. At least everybody in Macon, Georgia. He was about as contemporary as poetry got around Mercer. Anyway, all of my poems had very heavy sound devices. Unfortunately, though, they didn't make much sense. Then I met the Mississippi poet James Seay, who came to Mercer to do a reading. He'd just published his first book, *Let Not Your Hart*, from Wesleyan. Anyway, that was the first poetry reading I'd ever heard, and I was pretty impressed. I started reading his poems, which I liked very much, and we got to be friends. After a while, he put me onto Dickey's work. This may sound odd, but for years I didn't think Dickey was all that good. I see now that my judgment, or stupidity, or whatever, was a kind of safety mechanism, a defensive stance that allowed me to go on and write without that big shadow hovering over me. So, I never really felt intimidated by him. Also Dickey was much older than I was, a full generation.

Walsh: When did you first discover the real power of his work?

Bottoms: About the time I published my first book, I think. Or a few years before, the mid or late 70s, I suppose. Theodore Roethke was a huge influence on me then, especially the poems in *The Far Field*, and so was James Wright. I'm thinking of *The Branch Will Not Break* and *Shall We Gather at the River*. There were strong stories there, and wonderful language, and the poems were trying to reach for something other, something deeper. But this is hard, you know. I read a great deal back then, and there were tons of influences. Elizabeth Bishop was an early favorite. William Stafford was also important. And so were Phil Levine and Galway Kinnell. But Dickey was later. And Warren was later still.

Walsh: What was your relationship with Warren like?

Bottoms: Oh, I didn't really know him. After he chose *Shooting Rats* for the Whitman Award we swapped a letter or two, but I never got a chance to meet him. Well, I had two chances, but they both fell through. Once in the early eighties, when I was visiting Bennington, Dave Smith offered to drive me over to Warren's place in Connecticut, but Warren got sick. Then a few years later, when he was poet laureate, Warren invited me to read at the Library of Congress. He was to do the introduction, but he got sick again and couldn't make it. So I never got to meet him. I have to say though, that his work moves me more consistently than any other American poet. Years ago Dave Smith and I used to argue about who was the better poet—Warren or Dickey. I always stuck up for Dickey. Over the past few years, though, I've come to see a spiritual or philosophical dimension in Warren's poetry that Dickey possessed to a lesser degree. Dickey had a marvelous energy, and a wonderful gift for drama and language, but Warren's work, at least to me, has more spiritual depth.

Walsh: Are you speaking again about Warren's "yearning" for answers?

Bottoms: Yes, I suppose that's what strikes me about his work. I'm especially drawn to "Audubon" and those later poems. There's such a powerful and beautiful sense of consequence there. That's not to say there aren't touches of that all through his work, but it really seems to bloom in that last great spurt of energy. In his constant questioning of the world you see a philosophy develop that unites the whole body of his work.

Walsh: Thinking about Southern poetry as a whole, at least since the mid 20th century, what sort of patterns do you see and where do you see yourself in the mix of things?

Bottoms: Well, our first group of really fine poets was probably that Vanderbilt group—Ransom, Tate, Warren, Davidson, and later Randall Jarrell and Dickey. Out of that comes what we call Southern poetry, I suppose. Ernest Suarez has had a lot to say about this. He points out that contemporary Southern poetry has developed essentially into two lines— the narrative and the lyrical. The narrative line comes down through Warren and Dickey. I fall into that group, I suppose. Dave Smith would be a few years ahead of me there, and Rodney Jones and Andrew Hudgins almost exact contemporaries. On the other team you have Charles Wright, Ellen Voigt, Yusef Komunyakaa, who are Southern by birth but really follow another, more lyrical, tradition. But all of this is a simplification, of course. Each of these folks is certainly a mix. Even Charles Wright will sometimes break into a brief story. Still, there's a grain of truth there. No other poet I can think of, for instance, has Charles' pure gift for language, and if you asked Charles who his biggest influences were, I doubt that he'd point to any Southern writers.

Walsh: You've taught poetry writing for a number of years.

Bottoms: Twenty-five or so, I suppose.

Walsh: What the single greatest mistake you see young poets make?

Bottoms: That's very tough. I don't know if I'd call this a mistake, maybe a flaw. But so many poems I see by young writers, actually so many I see period, just don't have a sense of necessity about them. They don't communicate a compelling need to have been written. Either they memorialize some very uneventful event or they try to express some vague feeling the poet has had. They just never develop into art that carries the weight of necessity, of significance. And here's a thing too, especially about young poets. A large number of them, at least the ones I see, tend to confuse poetry and philosophy.

Walsh: You mean they want to write philosophy?

Bottoms: That's right. They want to write ideas and not poetry, and I'm of the old "show me, don't tell me" school. Students sometimes have trouble with that. Someone asked me once in a class, "Hey, but can't the poem be an idea?" I said no, absolutely not, and I stick by that. On the other hand, it can express an idea, and it usually will if it's any good. Karl Shapiro puts this well in an essay called "What is Not Poetry." He says, "If poetry has an opposite, it is philosophy. Poetry is a materialization of experience; philosophy is the abstraction of it." I love that, and it's a point I try to get across to all my students. Okay, think about this. Here's a story I like to tell. It's another simplification, sure, but it makes the point well enough for students. A poet and a philosopher are walking across Woodruff Park [in Atlanta], going over to Fairlie-Poplar for some Thai food. When they reach Peachtree Street they see a yellow flash go by, then hear a gigantic crash under the traffic light. A yellow MG has tried to beat the light and smashed into the side of a furniture truck. It's a mess. Well, the poet and the philosopher rush over and try to help. A crowd gathers, somebody's on a cell phone calling an ambulance. The driver of the MG has been thrown into the street. The sports car's a tangle of crushed metal. Gasoline, blood, and glass are everywhere. So, the philosopher takes it all in and immediately starts to abstract. He thinks "Accident, Chaos, Fate." The poet, on the other hand, whips out her notebook and writes down everything that happened. The yellow flash on Peachtree Street, the smell of the smoking brakes, the spilled gasoline, the sound of the impact, the blood in the street. She goes back to her apartment and fleshes it all out on a legal pad as vividly as she can, then she types it up into a poem, and sends it to *Five Points*. You get your copy a few months later and turn to a poem called "Smash Up." You read the poem. You ponder it for a few seconds. You think "Accident, Chaos, Fate." The point is this. The poet and the philosopher are both traveling to the same city. The poet is simply taking the scenic route. The poet is trying to make the world material on the page, so that the reader can abstract, so that the reader can take what clues the world offers and decipher meaning from them. The poet wants the reader to participate, to experience the event in a vivid way.

Walsh: You're trying to say that the poet's responsibility is to the world?

Bottoms: I'm trying to say that the world is what we have to work with, and what we're trying to make some sense out of. Before we can fathom out whatever sense there might be behind the world, we have to be true to the world itself. The poet, I think, should make the world accessible to the reader, should not simply tell the reader about the world, but as far as possible through the written word, the poet should allow the reader to experience the world. And, therefore, arrive first hand at whatever insights the world has to offer.

Walsh: This yearning for meaning that we were talking about, this searching for a significance beyond the physical world—I believe you said once in an essay that poetry is its most appropriate literary expression? Why is that?

Bottoms: Because it's the most intimate. I think it opens a door into the inner life, into the subconscious, more easily than other genres. And if there is some deeper significance, some spiritual Other, operating in the universe, it certainly doesn't operate in our lives in any rational way, but through the irrational. And here's where poetry helps. The act of poetry, both the reading and the writing of the poem, is a creative moment that gives us access to this part of ourselves, this inner life, and so makes us more available, I think, to the influence of this spiritual Other.

Walsh: I think that answer makes this last question almost superfluous, but I'll ask it anyway. I read not long ago, that if we had never invented poetry or if we never wrote another poem, it would make very little difference in the lives of most people. Do you agree or disagree?

Bottoms: Oh, I disagree very strongly. Without poetry, without art, I think we'd generally be much poorer spiritually. Even if a person doesn't read poetry, he or she benefits from a culture where other people do. Even if I don't go to museums and look at great paintings, I benefit in many ways because other people do. This is true because the human imagination is being exercised. Significant questions are being examined. The human imagination is turning them into art, and every piece of art we create is witness in some unique way to our humanity, our commonality. This is the way serious literature brings consequence into the world, and it exerts an influence that is powerfully contagious. It changes people's lives. We're affected not only individually, but collectively. Our very capacity for empathy and tenderness is being expanded.

INDEX